THE
Part-Time
VEGETARIAN

THE
Part-Time
VEGETARIAN

Louise Lambert-Lagacé
& Louise Desaulniers

Fitzhenry & Whiteside

The Part-Time Vegetarian
Copyright © 2003 Fitzhenry & Whiteside

Original title: Le végétarisme à temps partiel
Copyright © 2001 by Les éditions de l'Homme, une division du groupe Sogides

Fitzhenry & Whiteside
195 Allstate Parkway,
Markham, Ontario L3R 4T8

www.fitzhenry.ca   godwit@fitzhenry.ca

Fitzhenry & Whiteside acknowledges with thanks the Canada Council for the Arts, the Government of Canada through the Book Publishing Industry Development Program (BPIDP), and the Ontario Arts Council for their support for our publishing program.

    10 9 8 7 6 5 4 3 2 1

National Library of Canada Cataloguing in Publication

Lambert-Lagacé, Louise, 1941–
The part-time vegetarian: a flexible alternative to a strictly
vegetarian diet / Louise Lambert-Lagacé and Louise Desaulniers.

Translation of: Le végétarisme à temps partiel, by Louise Desaulniers and
Louise Lambert-Lagacé, published: Montréal : Éditions de l'Homme, 2001.
Includes bibliographical references and index.
ISBN 1-55005-057-5

1. Vegetarianism. 2. Vegetarian cookery. I. Desaulniers, Louise, dietitian
II. Title.

TX392.D4713 2003   613.2'62   C2003-900905-X

Text design : Tannice Goddard
Cover Design by: Darrell McCalla
Printed and bound in Canada

Contents

List of Tables

Acknowledgements

This book has been blessed with a number of great collaborators — and it is now enjoying its second life!

The inspiration for the book came from Louise Desaulniers's Healthy Fine Cuisine classes, which have been popular in Montreal for many years. Louise Desaulniers and Louise Lambert-Lagacé, partners and friends for many years, worked together to develop the book and shared the pleasure of bringing it to life. Other dietitians made important contributions along the way: Josée Thibodeau reviewed the plan and made excellent suggestions; Marie-Claire Garneau developed many of the delicious recipes; Ivanina Popova surveyed shops for new products and prepared the charts; Manon Lalonde, technician in dietetics, provided information on available vegetarian products. The book was then reviewed by critical and helpful readers: Janine Desrosiers Choquette, Micheline Lamarche, Michelle Laflamme, Pascale Lagacé, Sandrine Desaulniers, and Maryse Pallascio-Bigras.

The book's second life was made possible because of Nelson Doucet's interest in the topic and the commitment of Stoddart Publishing. Catherine Marjoribanks, our editor, has been a very patient and wonderful collaborator. Gillian Watts in

Toronto, Julie Desaulniers in Vancouver, and Pascale Lagacé in Edmonton compiled a list of healthy vegetarian products to make this book useful from coast to coast.

   Our deepest gratitude to these exceptional participants for helping us bring to life this very special book.

Note: From time to time, the authors refer to experiences from their own clinical practice. For the sake of efficiency, the abbreviation LLL refers to Louise Lambert-Lagacé, while LD refers to Louise Desaulniers.

"Part-Time Vegetarianism":
What Does It Really Mean?

Don't worry: this is definitely not a new fad diet! We could have called this book *How to Eat Less Meat*, but there is a whole lot more to it than that. We want to improve your menu by adding nutritional superstars. Part-time vegetarianism leads to a much healthier diet with more plant foods, more antioxidants, more micronutrients (boron, chromium, selenium, etc.). It has a lot in common with the traditional Mediterranean diet, which is light on meat and well known for its health benefits.

When we talk about "part-time vegetarianism," we are suggesting more flexibility than the traditional vegetarian diet. You decide how many meatless meals you want to add to your routine. You choose when to eat vegetarian meals:

- a few times a month, to familiarize yourself with delicious dishes based on legumes or tofu;
- two or three times a week, when you're in the mood to try new dishes;
- at suppertime, since a meatless menu is lighter and easier to digest; or
- most of the time, including fresh fish or grilled meat in the occasional meal.

*Part-time vegetarianism offers a unique opportunity to
discover new foods and flavours, add new textures to your meals,
and expand your recipe file. It can also improve your health.*

• • •

Why we wrote this book

Vegetarianism has long been seen as a strict diet, with some kind of philosophical, religious, or political component attached to it. It was sometimes seen as a "hippie" diet, and it was even regarded as "risky" by the medical profession. Thank goodness, this is no longer the case! Today, people of all ages are attracted to a meatless diet. Almost one-third of teenagers consider it "cool" to eat that way. More than 30 million North Americans have already tried a vegetarian diet, and baby boomers are now eating less and less meat. Why? It's a question of health. And it's also a question of taste.

Health threats associated with mad-cow disease and hoof-and-mouth are problems that worry us, but it wasn't fear that motivated our approach. It was the overwhelming scientific evidence demonstrating the benefits of plant foods that won us over and inspired us. Hardly a week goes by without more good news: tomatoes help to reduce the incidence of prostate cancer, soy and walnuts help to lower cholesterol, blueberries are exceptional antioxidants, and flaxseeds are a rich source of omega-3 fatty acids. The enhanced value of plant foods has brought vegetarianism in from the fringes and made it more attractive than ever. Many people count on plant foods to help them recover and maintain their health, and this type of diet is now specifically recommended to cardiac patients. The link between vegetarianism and good health has never been so strong.

And then there are the new flavours. With a vegetarian diet you can sample flavourful fruits and fresh vegetables, now available all year round, and discover soy products in many different and delicious forms. Food producers are getting the idea, too: supermarkets now offer whole-grain cereals and country-style breads, as well as new and tasty meatless products, cooked or frozen. And when you want an evening out, a wealth of ethnic restaurants welcome you to feast on hummus, fajitas, couscous, dhal, and a whole world of other interesting and delicious vegetarian dishes.

Vegetarian cooking has caught the imagination of some of the world's great chefs — like Georges Blanc in Burgundy, Normand Laprise in Montreal, Charlie Trotter in Chicago — who offer gourmet vegetarian dishes on their menus. Alain Passard, the chef at Arpège, a three-star restaurant in Paris's 7th arrondissement, no longer offers meat on his menu. "It was mainly a personal choice," he told the daily newspaper *Libération* in December 2000. "A chunk of meat no longer inspires me when vegetables are so much more colourful and tasty."

Unfortunately, vegetarianism is still not well understood as a nutritional system. Though bookstores are full of vegetarian cookbooks, few of them explain how to cut down on the meat in your diet without losing important nutritional value. Even people who are committed to vegetarianism don't know how to maintain a balanced diet.

Since 1990, Louise Desaulniers has been answering many of these questions in her course, offered at the Culinary Institute of Montreal, called "Healthy Fine Cuisine," which teaches techniques of menu-planning and cooking with legumes, tofu, whole grains, and greens. Every year, the course has attracted men and women of all ages who want to integrate vegetarian meals into their diet, but don't know how.

At our nutrition clinic — where we see patients in need of nutrition counselling to address problems that range from high cholesterol to breast cancer — we have also seen:

- parents who worry because their child refuses to eat a single bite of meat;
- teenagers who want to become vegetarians but have no idea how to find the nutrition they need in plant foods;
- men and women who have tried vegetarianism but find that they are frequently tired and experience sugar cravings;
- new vegetarians whose protein and iron levels have rapidly dropped;
- people suffering from high cholesterol who want to stop eating meat but only perpetuate their problem by eating cheese every day;
- people who have heard about the theory of "complementary protein" but who don't really understand it.

Although many experts have spoken out on the topic of healthy vegetarianism, there is still an obvious lack of practical information.

We want to share our knowledge so that you can improve your menu and include the right amount of protein at each meal, within a — more or less — vegetarian diet.

Of course, nutrition guidelines are important, but practical suggestions are essential. So we've included so many appetizing, easy-to-prepare recipes that we're sure you'll find some treasures here! Never again will you throw away that block of tofu because you don't know what to do with it.

With this book, you'll add winning dishes to
your menu and leave out meat without worry.

• • •

Different types of vegetarianism and health

The scientific evidence is unanimous: vegetarian eating provides great health benefits — if you go about it the right way. This means choosing the right foods and eating them at the right times. If you simply eat anything, any time, you'll be no better off than if you ate a non-vegetarian diet!

What is common to all types of vegetarianism is an abundance of plant foods, and that is their strong point. Different types of vegetarianism include other types of food, and the nutritional value of these diets depends on the entire range of foods being eaten regularly. If you leave out some of the key foods entirely, the nutritional value of your diet is decreased, which can lead to certain nutrient deficiencies and poor health. On the other hand, if your menu is balanced with a variety of key foods, you're likely to stay in good health. The same thing applies to a non-vegetarian diet.

The definitions below describe the strengths and weaknesses of the different types of vegetarianism.

"Strict" vegetarianism

Strict vegetarians eat plant products (cereals, legumes, nuts, seeds, fruits, and vegetables) exclusively. They add nothing to this common base of vegetarianism. Animal products and their derivatives are off the menu — no milk, yogurt, butter, honey, chicken broth, or gelatin. This is also called a **vegan** diet.

This type of diet contains little saturated fat, which is found mainly in meat and cheese, and no cholesterol, which is present only in foods of animal origin. It is rich in dietary fibre — which is excellent to prevent constipation — and provides vitamins and antioxidants, which are abundant in fruits, vegetables, and whole grains.

In the late 1980s, Dr. Dean Ornish of California used this type of vegetarianism in his treatment of patients with major cardiac problems, although he modified the menu slightly by adding egg whites and powdered skim milk. Ornish's study demonstrated that this type of diet could reverse heart disease (although it's worth noting that these patients also increased their physical activity and engaged in meditation).

However, strict vegetarianism puts severe limits on the variety of foods you can eat. According to a tried-and-true dictum of nutrition, the less variety on the menu, the higher the risk of nutrient deficiencies. At present, deficiencies due to a total absence of dairy products can be avoided because calcium, vitamin D, and vitamin B_{12} have been added to a number of soy and other cereal-based beverages, but strict vegetarians still have to know a great deal about nutrition, and may have to take the appropriate dietary supplements to avoid deficiencies.

Lacto-vegetarianism

In addition to plant foods, **lacto-vegetarians** eat dairy products, including milk, cheese, and yogurt. When we visited the small sacred city of Pushkar, India, in November 2000, we ate only lacto-vegetarian meals, as this was a religious law respected by hotel owners in the region. We tasted lovely combinations of vegetables, legumes, rice, yogurt, fresh cheese, different types of bread, and fresh fruits. We loved these flavourful dishes, and we ate our fill (between visits to the camel fair!).

Of course, a lacto-vegetarian diet includes a greater number of foods than a strict vegetarian menu, but it is healthy only if your food choices are. For example, if you drop the T-bone steak but choose fries and a bowl of ice cream instead, you are cutting out meat, but you aren't doing yourself any favours! You are getting a full ration of calcium and vitamin B_{12}, but at the same time you are clogging your arteries with a large dose of hydrogenated and saturated fat.

Lacto-ovo-vegetarianism

Lacto-ovo-vegetarians eat eggs and dairy products, in addition to the entire range of plant foods. The vast majority of Hindus, Trappist monks, and Seventh Day

Adventists are lacto-ovo-vegetarians, which means that this type of vegetarianism is practised by more than 90 percent of all vegetarians in the world. This diet does not present any particular nutritional risk — as long as the foods are properly chosen. It is often associated with a lower risk of heart disease, as are the other types of vegetarianism — though we must add that vegetarians usually have a healthier lifestyle than the general population.

In the clinic, we regularly see new lacto-ovo-vegetarians who don't know how to cook legumes or tofu; instead, they systematically replace meat with cheese. By doing this, they do not limit their intake of animal fat. They may even increase their cholesterol level and, eventually, develop an iron deficiency, since cheese and other dairy products don't provide enough of this essential nutrient.

A long-time lacto-ovo-vegetarian who had weight and cholesterol problems consulted us at the clinic. An evaluation of this woman's menu revealed that she ate a lot of cheese, homemade cakes, and muffins, but few plant foods such as vegetables, legumes, or soy products. Her food choices had perpetuated her weight and cholesterol problems. In this case, it was the *application* of vegetarianism that was at fault.

Semi-vegetarianism

More and more people have dropped red meat and cold cuts but keep poultry and fish in their diet. They are not vegetarians in the strict sense of the term, but they are often called **semi-vegetarians**. These semi-vegetarians don't necessarily eat huge amounts of vegetables, fruits, and cereals, but they do consume dairy products, eggs, poultry, and fish on a regular basis. The health benefit in this type of diet arises from a greater intake of plant foods and fish but is not related to simply replacing beef with chicken.

Part-time vegetarianism

Finally, you might not fit into any category, or follow any specific theory: you might just want to improve your menu, add more plant foods, eat lighter meals, enjoy fish and seafood, or replace meat with legumes or tofu from time to time. We are pleased to say that we have made a new category for you: the **part-time vegetarian**.

This less formal style of vegetarianism does not impose any rules but allows you to improve your eating habits and discover new and nutritious foods. Again, the choice and the distribution of foods throughout the day are the cornerstone of a successful menu.

The traditional Mediterranean diet

This type of diet — a form of part-time vegetarianism — was seen in the 1950s among populations living near the Mediterranean Sea. It is now being studied — and praised — by nutritionists around the world.

Based on fresh foods, the Mediterranean diet contains a lot more fruits, vegetables, whole grains, nuts, and legumes than the usual North American diet. It includes yogurt and cheese, olive oil and fish, and much less meat and fewer sweets. This type of diet increases life expectancy because it includes more substances that protect the heart and arteries, such as omega-3 fatty acids, antioxidants, and B-complex vitamins. It is associated with a lower risk of heart disease, while North American menus have the opposite effect.

The famous Lyon Diet Heart Study used the Mediterranean diet model in treating people who had suffered a heart attack. The study clearly demonstrated that the risk of recurrence after a first infarctus could be reduced by 70 percent with a diet richer in cereals, grains, fruits, leafy green vegetables, and fish. No study using medication has had such a striking protective effect.

> *No matter what kind of vegetarianism you're interested in, you'll always be ahead when you eat more vegetables, fruits, legumes, soy and soy products, cereals, whole-grain products, nuts, and seeds. Always keep this in mind!*
>
> • • •

An approach that works for everyone

Whether you are over sixty, under thirty, or somewhere in between, whether you have young children or teenagers to feed, whether you're pregnant or nursing, a well-balanced, mainly vegetarian menu can provide proper nutrition. It can even help prevent or treat heart problems, diabetes, and hypertension and reduce the risk of cancer (see Chapter 8).

You can't learn to be a vegetarian overnight, but you won't make many mistakes if you respect certain nutritional guidelines.

Children can grow and develop normally without eating meat if they take in enough calories and proteins. If a child is a strict vegetarian, his or her intake of vitamins B_{12} and D must be monitored carefully and supplemented if necessary. If a child is a part-time vegetarian and eats a bit of everything, there is no need to worry.

In adolescence, vegetarianism sometimes coincides with the onset of bulimia and anorexia. Although it isn't the cause of such problems, it becomes an excuse for limiting food intake. If this happens, and especially if the teenager is a strict vegetarian, consulting with a dietitian can be useful. In other cases, a mostly vegetarian menu is compatible with normal growth, but foods rich in iron (see Chapter 2, Table 3) and calcium should be encouraged.

A vegetarian menu can also meet the nutritional needs of pregnant and nursing women. Well-nourished vegetarian women can give birth to babies of normal weight. In the case of strict vegetarian women, supplements of vitamins B_{12} and D are essential during pregnancy and nursing.

Even competitive athletes can fulfil their nutritional needs while eating a vegetarian menu if they include enough foods rich in both plant and animal protein. This is exactly what we encourage in part-time vegetarianism.

A menu that is higher in plant foods but also includes some animal foods can meet everyone's nutritional needs, especially when this menu features nutritional superstars:

- leafy green vegetables, the green-pea family, the cabbage family, carrots, and winter squashes
- seasonal fruits, including citrus fruits, berries, melons, mangoes, and kiwi fruit
- whole grains, including brown rice, quinoa, millet, amaranth, and pot barley
- whole-grain cereal products, from bread to whole-wheat pasta, buckwheat (kasha), and brown rice
- legumes, from lentils to chickpeas
- soy, including soy beverages, tofu, and roasted soybeans
- nuts and seeds, including walnuts, flaxseeds, and natural nut butters
- dairy products, such as milk, yogurt, kefir, fresh cheeses, and ripened cheeses

- eggs and poultry (grain-fed when possible), fresh meats, and organ meats
- fish, whether caught wild or farmed, seafood, and molluscs
- a moderate amount of fat, such as olive, canola, sesame, or hazelnut oil
- a variety of seasonings, such as herbs and spices

With all of these foods on your menu, you'll be hitting the target of good nutrition. And if you have access to fresh foods, whole-grain cereal products, and organic foods, you are adding quality and flavour.

A mostly vegetarian menu is good for you at any age.

• • •

2

Guidelines to Follow
for a Balanced Diet

Maintaining a balanced diet is always a challenge, but following a few simple guidelines will help you to curb hunger pangs, sugar cravings, and fatigue, as well as give you protection against anemia. These guidelines, which can be used in both vegetarian and non-vegetarian diets, call on you to take into account two very important nutrients: protein and iron.

First guideline: Eat enough protein at each meal

One can survive without meat, but one cannot survive without protein. Nevertheless, you don't need to adopt a high-protein diet to have the appropriate amount of protein at each meal.

An eleven-year-old girl who had started a vegetarian diet came to see LD with her mother. The girl had cut meat from her diet, ate little fish, and was not enjoying legumes or tofu. She was always tired, could not function normally, and was as pale as a ghost. It was obvious that her menu lacked protein. The girl's mother supported her decision and was ready to try cooking new dishes. In order to regain her energy, the girl agreed to taste tofu-based meals, eat fish more often, and learn about other good sources of protein. She soon felt the difference!

How much protein is appropriate varies according to a person's age, size, healthy weight, state of health, and physical activity. A small, not very active person will need less protein than a tall and athletic individual. Pregnant and nursing women need more protein than normal, of course. If you are recovering from surgery or cancer treatment, a higher intake of protein will help repair tissue and allow growth of new tissue. If you are over sixty, your needs are even higher than they were when you were thirty.

Calculating your protein needs isn't that complicated. On average, your needs correspond to **slightly less than one gram of protein per kilogram of healthy weight.**

To find out your weight in kilograms, divide your weight in pounds by 2.2. For example, if you weigh 125 pounds, you divide 125 by 2.2 to obtain your weight in kilograms: 57 kg. At this weight, 50 grams of protein per day is considered an appropriate amount if you aren't very active physically.

I. YOUR PROTEIN NEEDS VARY ACCORDING TO YOUR SITUATION

They are slightly greater

- before or after surgery
- during cancer treatment
- during pregnancy
- when you are over sixty

Needs rise by 50%
during intensive athletic training

The appropriate amount determined by our simplified formula does not correspond to a maximum daily intake of protein. If you add a few grams, it won't do you any harm. But if you never reach your target amount, you run the risk of feeling tired and having other problems associated with a protein deficiency.

> A woman who had made major dietary changes — she had more or less given up meat — consulted LLL. After three months on her own new diet, she was feeling increasingly fatigued. Her intake of protein was below 30 grams per day, which was equivalent to one-half of her needs. Blood tests revealed a noticeable lack of protein. When she made the necessary adjustments, her energy returned.

Note: 50 grams of protein is not the same thing as 50 grams of meat. Grams of protein are invisible and cannot be weighed on the butcher's scale. For example, a chicken breast or fish filet contains at least 20 grams of protein; an egg has 5 grams; and a slice of whole-wheat bread contains less than 3 grams. The table on the next page shows the protein content of various foods.

> Vegetables contain little protein and cannot make a significant contribution to the minimum intake required — 15 grams — in a meal. A large serving of vegetables, 250 ml (1 cup), contains only 2 to 5 grams of protein. That is why we have not calculated the protein content of vegetables in our model menus. Fruits contain no protein at all.
>
> Cereal products such as bread, pasta, rice, and quinoa contain some protein, but the quantity cannot significantly contribute to the 15-gram minimum intake needed at each meal. For example, a slice of whole-wheat bread contains 2 to 3 grams of protein, while 250 ml (1 cup) of legumes provides 15 grams.

Enough protein at each meal . . .

Leaving meat out of your meal won't cause you any problems . . . but don't leave out the protein! If you don't get enough protein at breakfast, you tend to have

2. GOOD SOURCES OF PROTEIN

Legumes and other plant sources

The amount given is a cooked portion of 250 ml (1 cup) unless otherwise indicated.
Values are given in grams of protein.

Soybeans	30
White beans	21
Lentils	19
Split peas	17
Red beans	17
Black beans	16
Lima beans	16
Chickpeas	15
Mung beans	15
Tofu, regular, 100 g (3 1/2 oz)	15
Tofu, silken, 170 g (6 oz)	13
Roasted soybeans, 30 g (1 oz)	11
Soy beverage, 300 ml (1 1/4 cups)	8
Peanut or nut butter, 15 ml (1 tbsp)	5
Almonds or walnuts, 45 ml (3 tbsp)	5
Hummus, 45 ml (3 tbsp)	5

Animal sources

The amount given is a cooked portion of 60 g (2 oz) unless otherwise indicated.
Values are given in grams of protein.

Chicken breast (without skin)	18
Pork shoulder	17
Salmon	16
Lean chopped beef	16
Cottage or ricotta cheese, 125 ml (1/2 cup)	15
Yogurt, 250 ml (1 cup)	10
Cheddar-type hard cheese, 45 g (1 1/2 oz)	11
Milk, 3.5%, 2%, 1%, or skim, 250 ml (1 cup)	9
Egg, 1 medium	5

energy drops before lunchtime; a light meal at lunch or a lunch rich in starchy foods leads to sugar cravings around four in the afternoon, a ravenous appetite at supper, and a few snack attacks during the evening. Far too many people eat this way and do not realize that, to function properly, the body needs protein at regular intervals; this maintains a good level of energy, stabilizes blood-sugar levels, and prevents hunger pangs and exhaustion at the end of the day. The best times to take in adequate protein are at breakfast and lunch — but that's not how most people eat.

At the clinic we see so many problems associated with the poor distribution of protein throughout the day that we give this issue a great deal of attention in menu planning.

Menu problems

If we are aiming for a daily intake of 50 grams of protein, balanced throughout the day, we can see that many menus contain too little protein in the morning and at noon and way too much protein at night. The imbalance is obvious and common. In the typical menus below, foods with protein content are highlighted in boldface type. (For more detail, see Table 2, p. 14.)

Breakfast:	bread, jam, and coffee (0 g protein)
Lunch:	vegetable soup, pita bread, small **yogurt** (5 g protein)
Supper:	**grilled fish**, vegetables, bread and **cheese, crème caramel** (45 g protein)

Breakfast:	muffin and coffee (2–3 g protein)
Lunch:	**millet pie**, apple (6 g protein)
Supper:	**grilled half chicken**, rice, Caesar salad, **yogurt** (40 g protein)

Breakfast:	cereal and **milk**, coffee (8 g protein)
Lunch:	tomato sandwich, apple (0 g protein)
Supper:	**steak** (170 g, or 6 oz), mixed vegetables, **rice pudding** (40 g protein)

Breakfast: 3 or 4 fresh fruits (0 g protein)
Lunch: bean sprouts, **hard-boiled egg**, tomato, crackers (5 g protein)
Supper: rice with **shrimp** and mixed vegetables, **yogurt** (20 g protein)

Breakfast: bagel and cream cheese, **café au lait** (5 g protein)
Lunch: green salad, raw vegetables, **vegetarian spread**, multigrain
                bread (5 g protein)
Supper: vegetable couscous, marinated **seitan**, fresh fruits (7 g protein)

> **Seitan** is made with wheat protein extracted from semolina flour. This gluten
> dough is cooked in a broth seasoned with soy sauce and algae. Contrary to
> popular belief, seitan is not a good source of protein. It should not be
> confused with **tempeh**, which is made of soybeans and *is* a good source of
> protein (see p. 36).

Many people mistakenly believe that certain popular vegetarian foods — such as
millet pie, vegetarian spread, sprouts, and seitan — are good sources of protein.
Unfortunately, they aren't, so if you like to eat these foods, be sure to add a good
source of protein to your meal as well.

Menu improvements

For a truly balanced diet, you must spread protein-rich foods over all three meals.
Make sure you get enough protein at breakfast and lunch, especially; these are the
most important meals.

Keeping in mind that you need at least **15 grams of protein per meal**, consult
Table 2 to find out how many grams of protein various foods contain.

The following menus have been designed to provide a better distribution of
protein, even though there is only one meal per day containing meat, poultry, or
fish.

Breakfast: fresh fruit, **soy** cereal, **milk** (15 g protein)
Lunch: **lentil** salad, **feta** cheese, whole-wheat pita, fruit (15 g protein)
Supper: **grilled chicken**, brown rice, green vegetables, fruit gelatin
                (15 g protein)

Breakfast:	bowl of **yogurt**, 20 chopped **nuts**, fresh fruit (15 g protein)
Lunch:	**tuna** and greens, whole-wheat bread, fresh fruit (15 g protein)
Supper:	**chickpea** stew, broccoli, fruit compote (15 g protein)

Breakfast:	two slices of rye bread, **peanut butter**, **café au lait** (15 g protein)
Lunch:	scrambled **tofu**, stir-fried vegetables, pita, **yogurt** (15 g protein)
Supper:	rice with **shrimp** and mixed vegetables, fresh fruit (15 g protein)

These are not the "rabbit-food" menus with mountains of leafy vegetables that many people think of when they hear the word "vegetarian." Why? Because rabbit foods such as carrots and greens supply very little protein.

To be certain that you are always getting the right amount of protein, consult Table 2. If you buy ready-to-serve meals, check the labels to find out about their protein content per serving and add other protein-rich foods to your meal, if needed (see the Appendix, p.163). And for some delicious ideas, try the 25 menus at the end of this book.

The notion of protein complementarity revisited

Proteins present in legumes, nuts, and cereal products aren't exactly the same as those in meat, poultry, eggs, and soybeans. The former are called "incomplete" proteins, while the latter are called "complete." This reality has existed since the dawn of time, but thirty years ago, the idea of eating complementary plant proteins — bringing together two incomplete proteins in the same meal — was born. Frances Moore Lappé, an early proponent of this approach, made menu planning complicated, and so it made people anxious about what they ate. Surprisingly, the theory survives today, even though experts in the field discredited it years ago.

It is not necessary to eat a cereal product and a legume at the same meal, even though many menus lend themselves to this combination. The accepted approach, which is simpler to understand and follow, is to eat different plant proteins every day — legumes, soy products, nuts, and cereals; this approach will satisfy the needs of strict vegetarians. Part-time vegetarians don't have to follow this approach, since their menu is planned around a variety of protein of both animal and plant origin.

*Be sure to include an adequate amount of protein in your diet every day,
and remember: at least 15 grams of protein at each meal is the key to a
balanced diet and energy from morning to night.*

• • •

Second guideline: Eat enough iron-rich foods

Iron is extremely important to good health. Carried by the red blood cells, iron transports oxygen and stores it in the muscles, evacuates carbon dioxide to the lungs, and serves other vital functions. Individuals who lack iron suffer from anemia, which leads to symptoms ranging from an inability to concentrate to a weakened immune system. Anemia is widespread among both vegetarians and non-vegetarians throughout the world when there isn't enough iron in the daily diet or when it is poorly absorbed. Women before menopause suffer more from a lack of iron than do men, due mainly to losses during menstruation. Children are also a very vulnerable group.

To prevent this situation, the recommended daily intake for women was recently increased from 14 milligrams to 18 milligrams per day by the committee of experts that periodically reviews nutritional recommendations for Canada and the United States. The recommended daily intake for men is still 8 milligrams per day. Because the iron in plant foods is less well absorbed than the iron in animal flesh, the dose recommended for **strict vegetarians** goes up to 36 milligrams per day for women before menopause and 16 milligrams per day for postmenopausal women and for men of all ages. You can see why it's important to include iron-rich foods and foods that encourage iron absorption on a daily basis.

Among the richest sources of iron are iron-fortified breakfast cereals; organ meats, such as liver and kidneys; legumes, such as soybeans; molluscs, such as oysters, mussels, and clams; and blackstrap molasses. As you can see, red meat is not the only source.

Iron needs two key helpers to be well absorbed

A part-time vegetarian diet favours iron absorption. In fact, our approach — designed around a regular intake of foods rich in vitamin C and a minimum intake of animal flesh — allows the key helpers to improve iron absorption.

3. GOOD SOURCES OF IRON

Plant sources

The amount given is a cooked portion of 250 ml (1 cup) unless otherwise indicated.
Values are given in milligrams.

Soybeans	9
White beans	8
Lentils	7
Chickpeas	5
Tofu, regular, 100 g (3 1/2 oz)	5
Black-eyed peas	4
Lima beans	4
Split peas	3
Tofu, silken, firm, 170 g (6 oz)	1.8

Fruits and vegetables

Spinach	6
1 medium-sized potato	3
5 dried figs	2

Animal sources

The amount given is a cooked portion of 90 g (3 oz).
Values are given in milligrams.

Atlantic oysters (raw)	17
Pork liver	15
Veal, beef, or chicken liver	7
Mussels or octopus	6
Trout (grilled)	2
Lean chopped beef	2
Lamb or rabbit	2
Stewing veal	1
Chicken breast	0.9
Pork loin	0.7

Daily nutritional intake recommended by the National Academy of Sciences in 2001:
• Woman before menopause: 18 milligrams
• Postmenopausal women and all men: 8 milligrams
• Strict vegetarian men and postmenopausal women: 16 milligrams
• Strict vegetarian women before menopause: 36 milligrams

1. A constant intake of foods rich in vitamin C

Vitamin C acidifies the gastric environment and enables iron to remain soluble, which doubles or even triples its availability for absorption. Including at least 75 milligrams of vitamin C in the form of fruits and vegetables in each meal is important — and it's simple. In the menus below, the foods in boldface type are good sources of vitamin C. Some of these menus do not have enough vitamin C, while others do.

Breakfast:
- cereal with milk and nuts, coffee (0 mg of vitamin C)
- toast, peanut butter, apple, café au lait (5 mg of vitamin C)
- **orange juice** or **half a grapefruit**, cereal, milk, coffee (75 mg of vitamin C)
- **kiwi fruit** or **half cantaloupe**, bowl of yogurt and nuts, café au lait (75 mg of vitamin C)

Lunch or supper:
- green salad, grilled chicken, brown rice, pear or apple (20 mg of vitamin C)
- **tomato juice, coleslaw**, grilled chicken, whole-grain bread, pear (75 mg of vitamin C)
- half **green pepper**, chickpea salad, whole-grain bread, 2 **clementines** (100 mg of vitamin C)
- **cauliflower** and dip, grilled trout, steamed carrots and **broccoli**, whole-grain bread, peach (85 mg of vitamin C)
- raw vegetables, hearty lentil soup, whole-grain bread, **kiwi fruit** (75 mg of vitamin C)

4. EXAMPLES OF FOOD COMBINATIONS HIGH IN VITAMIN C

One portion is 250 ml (1 cup) unless otherwise indicated.
Values are given in milligrams.

Food	Vitamin C	Total
Half grapefruit	43	
Kale	56	99

4. EXAMPLES OF FOOD COMBINATIONS HIGH IN VITAMIN C (cont.)

One portion is 250 ml (1 cup) unless otherwise indicated.
Values are given in milligrams.

Food	Vitamin C	Total
Honeydew melon	45	
Tomato juice	47	92
Cranberry juice	40	
Asparagus	50	90
Fresh currants	49	
Spinach	40	89

5. GOOD SOURCES OF VITAMIN C

One portion is 250 ml (1 cup) unless otherwise indicated.
Values are given in milligrams.

Fruits and fruit juices

Blackcurrants	202
1 medium papaya, peeled	188
1 medium guava	165
Fresh orange juice	131
Orange juice, frozen, reconstituted	102
Fresh strawberries	89
Apricot nectar, vitamin C added	88
Unsweetened pineapple juice, vitamin C added	87
Unsweetened apple juice, vitamin C added	87
Grapefruit juice, frozen, reconstituted	83
1 kiwi fruit	75
Cantaloupe, cubed	71
10 litchi nuts	70
1 orange	70
1 mango	57
Fresh currants	49
Passionfruit juice	45

5. GOOD SOURCES OF VITAMIN C (cont.)

One portion is 250 ml (1 cup) unless otherwise indicated.
Values are given in milligrams.

Fruits and fruit juices

Honeydew melon	45
Half grapefruit, white or pink	43
Cranberry juice, vitamin C added	40

Vegetables and vegetable juices

Red or green bell pepper	160
Brussels sprouts, cooked	102
Broccoli, cooked or raw	100
Kohlrabi, cooked or raw	93
Kale, raw	85
Snow peas, cooked	81
Cauliflower, cooked or raw	75
Vegetable juice	71
Kale, cooked	56
Asparagus, cooked	50
Tomato juice	47
Bok-choy, cooked	44
Green or red cabbage	43
Spinach, cooked	40

Daily nutritional intake recommended by the National Academy of Sciences in 2001:
Women: 75 milligrams
Men: 90 milligrams

2. A small amount of animal flesh

Eating just a small amount of animal flesh at a meal can increase iron absorption by 200 to 400 percent — this is called the "meat factor." If the meal includes only 30 g (1 oz) of fish, chicken, or seafood mixed with other foods, the iron is better absorbed than if that small amount of animal flesh is not present. The meat factor does not apply when the meal features eggs or cheese.

Even if you do not eat animal flesh at each meal, as a part-time vegetarian, you can eat it from time to time, thus increasing iron retention compared to a person whose menu never contains fish, chicken, or meat.

Some conditions impede absorption of iron, such as consumption of tea or milk with the meal. On the other hand, researchers have found that having adequate vitamin C at these same meals neutralizes these negative effects. In fact, the intake of an adequate quantity of vitamin C makes all the difference.

It is important to eat enough iron-rich foods and never to neglect their perfect partners at each meal: fruits and vegetables high in vitamin C.

• • •

3

Meatless Meals: Easier Than You Think!

Instead of telling you what not to eat, a mostly vegetarian diet comes with a list of new and interesting foods for you to try. To make the switch while optimizing the benefits, go slowly.

Making gradual changes

If you want to leave meat or poultry out of your menu most days, do it gradually, and plan a transition period to expand your repertoire of recipes. It's important to give your digestive system time to adjust. Minor changes are easy to handle but major changes can cause trouble. One enthusiastic woman who took a nutrition course added so many raw vegetables to her diet in one week that she complained of terrible stomach aches for a week afterwards. This is only one example, but the fact is, the body doesn't like sudden changes. It can object quite strongly and make you regret your new eating pattern, even if it is a very healthy one! The wisest move is to take it step by step.

Start by learning more about legumes and soy products. If you haven't been eating or cooking with these foods, it will take a little while for you to become familiar with them. Take a month or two to feel physically and mentally comfortable with your new diet.

Here are some suggestions that can help you make the change:

- Make a list of the foods and meals that you usually eat and check off the ones that have legumes or soy products in them — tofu spaghetti sauce, lentil soup, chickpea salad, and so on. If you eat these foods a few times a month, plan to serve them a little more often.
- If you don't have recipes that fit the bill, take a second look around your super-market, and head for the section that offers legumes, canned or sold in bulk. Then, check the different kinds of tofu that are available: regular or silken. Make a list of the possibilities open to you.
- Reduce the amount of meat in your favourite recipes by replacing some of the minced beef with crumbled tofu or cooked lentils; it's easy to do, especially when you're making spaghetti sauce or shepherd's pie.
- If legumes have never been a part of your diet, don't eat a full serving the first time, since it might cause gas and fermentation (see "The issue of flatulence or gas," p. 58). In the long run, the more legumes you eat, the less your body will react.
- Try one new recipe every week (see "The 25 Menus and Their Recipes," p. 61). If the people you're cooking for think it's a hit, keep it in a file. It's always easier to prepare the second time round! You can even double the recipe and store half in the freezer.
- Try the new soy-based foods that imitate meat or cheese — you'll find quite a variety at the supermarket — and make a note of your favourites (see pp. 36 and 38).

For fruits and vegetables, make a list of your favourites and check it against the list of those rich in vitamin C (see Table 5, pp. 21 and 22). Plan your menu so that you have a fruit or vegetable high in vitamin C with each meal.

Time-saving tips

The top time-saving tip is to have tasty ingredients on hand. Vegetarian dishes become exciting when they include a clever blend of spices, fragrant fresh herbs, and tangy relishes or chutneys. Seasonings provide colour, flavour, and personality to your cuisine and become a key to your success.

The essentials: Keep your pantry well stocked with spices (such as cumin, coriander seed, nutmeg, cinnamon, allspice, cardamom, curry powder, and ginger) and dried herbs (such as thyme, tarragon, basil, chives, coriander, parsley, marjoram, rosemary, mint, and savory), so you won't be disappointed or have to run to the store at the last minute. If fresh herbs are available — such as thyme, basil, or chives — use them, because they're even tastier.

Among other basic ingredients to have on hand are light tamari sauce, which contains less salt (see Table 7, p. 37), extra-virgin olive oil, homemade or store-bought tomato sauce, homemade or store-bought pesto, wine and balsamic vinegars, Dijon mustard, fresh garlic, various chutneys, black or white sesame seeds,flaxseeds and sunflower seeds, nuts (almonds, pistachios, walnuts, and hazelnuts), unsalted roasted soybeans (see p. 34), miso (see p. 38), ready-to-serve vegetable and chicken broths (the best are from Pacific and Imagine), and fresh lemons. With these ingredients, a whole world of interesting, exciting recipes is at your fingertips.

At harvest time, store summer delicacies by making ketchup and tomato and fruit chutneys. They'll add a swirl of texture and flavour to legume and tofu dishes.

The staples: The staples of vegetarian cooking are, of course, dried or canned legumes such as red, green, and brown lentils and split peas, along with a variety of canned legumes such as red and white beans, chickpeas, black beans, romano beans, and soybeans. If you always have some in the pantry, you'll always have the makings of a meal!

Other ingredients you'll want to keep on hand are vacuum-sealed silken tofu, which can be kept in the cupboard for months, whole grains such as brown basmati rice, which is so much tastier than ordinary brown rice, long-cooking rolled oats, whole-wheat pastry flour, and whole-wheat pasta.

As your repertoire of recipes grows, so will the variety of legumes, whole grains, nuts, herbs, and spices that you'll use. And your dining pleasure will improve by leaps and bounds!

Ready-to-serve foods: You can find a variety of ready-to-serve vegetarian foods in the supermarket. They're great when you're in a hurry (see "Other supermarket minute foods," p. 30) and don't have time to cook from scratch.

Here are some foods that will help you out in a pinch:

- Hummus — a well-known spiced purée of chickpeas from the Middle East — is available in all grocery stores, and it's a hit with children and teens. Spread 125 ml (1/2 cup) on a whole-wheat pita, azim bread (a flat or unleavened bread), or a corn tortilla, and top it off with grated carrots, chopped greens, or fresh coriander. Roll it up like a vegetarian wrap for a tasty meal on the go.
- Chicken- and beef-flavour soy burgers are widely available in supermarket refrigerator sections (see Appendix, p. 163). It takes just a few minutes to heat them in a microwave oven or in a pan. Crumble them up and add them to a tomato-and-vegetable spaghetti sauce, or to rice with vegetables, for extra protein. Or simply serve them in whole-wheat hamburger buns garnished with sliced tomatoes, lettuce, or watercress, and spiced with a bit of salsa or homemade ketchup, as part of a fast and easy vegetarian meal.
- Amy's brand tofu and vegetarian lasagnas are available in individual and family sizes at many supermarkets. Ready to eat in a half-hour, they're always popular with the teen set. They're a good source of protein and taste great with salad. Add yogurt and fruit or a glass of milk for a complete meal.
- Commensal's tofu fricassee is not available everywhere in Canada. It can be served with steamed vegetables, a ratatouille, or stir-fried vegetables. Serve it with brown rice or whole-grain bread, a green salad, and fruit. It's a quick, delicious meal.

Meal-in-a-bowl soups: On weekends, when everyone has more time, get your family into the kitchen to prepare a legume and vegetable soup. It's fun for everyone — and a great way to get the kids interested in cooking. You'll be glad to have this type of soup on hand for quick and nutritious lunches or suppers. Use Bean Cuisine's soup packets, which contain ingredients for a substantial, nutritious soup: legumes, dried herbs, and a super blend of spices. Simply add garlic, onions, carrots, celery, or other chopped vegetables, along with olive oil and chicken or vegetable broth, and simmer for a couple of hours. The results are very tasty, and can fill twelve to fifteen bowls. Once the soup has cooled, you can freeze it in meal-size portions.

If you want something even quicker to prepare, add one or two cans of cooked legumes to homemade vegetable soup and simmer long enough for the flavours to blend. When you're almost ready to eat, add fresh spinach, Swiss chard, or beet leaves. Cook just enough to soften the leaves. For added taste, stir in a tablespoon of pesto before you add the greens, and sprinkle with freshly grated Parmesan.

A completely different vegetarian pizza: Buy a whole-wheat pizza crust and garnish it at home. Spread on tomato sauce, or cover it with thin slices of fresh Italian tomatoes (in season), then top it off with colourful vegetables: flowerets of blanched broccoli, rounds of red, green, or yellow bell peppers, thin slices of zucchini, sliced mushrooms, spinach leaves, and a few sliced black olives. Instead of pepperoni, use soy-based wieners that have been steamed for a few minutes — count one sausage per person. Cut each sausage lengthwise and arrange them attractively on the vegetables. Sprinkle with grated mozzarella or an Italian-flavour soy simulated cheese for people with a lactose intolerance. This pizza is much richer in vegetables and proteins than commercial vegetarian pizzas.

Enriched tomato sauce: To thicken a tomato sauce, add small red lentils ten to fifteen minutes before it has finished cooking: the lentils won't really change the taste of the sauce but will significantly enhance its nutritional value and improve the texture.

Vegetarian stuffed peppers: Instead of stuffing peppers with minced beef, mix tomato sauce and cooked lentils with leftover brown basmati rice, stuff the peppers with this mixture, and bake. Simple, easy, and delicious.

The incredible wok meal: Cooking with a wok is easy — and you can sample dishes from around the world! With a flip of the wrist, you can whip up a meal with an Asian, Eastern, or Provençal flavour. Sauté three or four colourful vegetables — such as broccoli, snow peas, bell peppers of all colours, or asparagus — and add cubes of herb-flavoured tofu or cooked legumes, and cashew nuts or almonds. Season with a broth spiced with cumin and curry, black olives and sun-dried tomatoes, or light tamari sauce, fresh ginger, and sesame seeds. Serve with brown rice, quinoa — a whole grain that cooks like rice — or whole-wheat pasta.

Stock up the freezer: Dishes prepared with legumes freeze very well, so go ahead and cook large quantities, then freeze portions for last-minute suppers.

Simple ways to include soy in your meals:
- Use fortified soy beverage on breakfast cereals instead of milk; it's creamy and has a mild taste.
- Cook oatmeal or cream of wheat in soy beverage instead of water or milk.
- Add unflavoured soy beverage to homemade soups for a smoother texture.
- Add crunch to a salad or casserole dish with a sprinkle of unsalted roasted soybeans (see p. 34).
- For an elegant, **quick dessert** from your blender or food processor, whip together a package of silken tofu with a bag of thawed frozen strawberries, raspberries, or blueberries, a bit of lemon zest, and a drop of maple syrup. Serve in your best glass dessert bowls. No one will ever guess that this delectable treat is made with tofu!

Different breakfasts: Try **creamed tofu with bananas**. It's quick and easy. In the blender, place half a package or 170 g (6 oz) of silken tofu, a large, ripe banana, the juice of half a lemon, and three generous tablespoons of plain yogurt; blend until creamy — it won't take a minute. To increase the fibre and good omega-3 fat content, add 15 ml (1 tbsp) of ground flaxseeds with the other ingredients. Add a few berries on top and enjoy!

Other supermarket minute foods

New meatless preparations appear in the supermarket every week. The range of soy-based and legume products has never been so varied and delicious (see Appendix, p. 163).

When you decide to buy a ready-made main dish, make sure that the product you choose has 15 to 20 grams of protein per portion. Always read the label to check the protein content, since many products that are called main dishes often contain only 5 to 10 grams of protein per portion.

You'll find in the refrigerated section of supermarkets, among other things,

- Yves Veggie Cuisine products, which are made with soy protein and generally contain 15 to 20 grams of protein per portion: vege-burgers, sliced simulated pepperoni and simulated turkey, simulated smoked sausages (spicy or mild), and tofu lasagnas. In addition, this company offers simulated cheese in Italian, Swiss, and other flavours, made with casein and soybeans, packed in individually wrapped slices — just like Kraft! Each slice contains 4 grams of protein and can be used like real cheese on pizzas, in cooked dishes, and in sandwiches.

The frozen-food sections of supermarkets and natural-foods stores offer, among other things,

- Amy's products, which include a wide range of organic vegetarian foods: tofu and vegetable-and-cheese lasagna, tasty pizzas with or without cheese, various burgers and whole-grain- and legume-based dishes. The protein content varies, and not all dishes contain the appropriate 15 to 20 grams of protein. Read the label carefully or increase the portions, if needed.
- Soyaganic, which is baked tofu in blocks with a sauce — Italian, teriyaki, or Szechuan style.

Some canned and dried products you'll find are

- Canned meal-in-a-bowl bean soups from Health Valley, Amy's, and Shari Ann's, and dried main-dish soups by Fantastic, which supply about 10 grams of protein per portion. Most of these soups are based on legumes and vegetables. Health Valley also makes a black-bean vegetarian chili with 14 grams of protein per portion.
- Products by Eden Foods, known for their organic canned legumes, also include canned bean soups containing 10 grams of protein per portion.

Stock up on these products for the days when you're in a rush. Simply add fresh vegetables, steamed or in a salad, a whole-grain product, and fruit, and your meat-less meal will never be lacking in colour, taste, or nutritional value. Add yogurt for dessert, if the protein content is not adequate.

4

The Different Faces of Soy

Soybeans are very different from chickpeas, lentils, and all the other legumes. That's why they deserve a separate chapter.

Unlike other legumes, soybeans quietly slipped into North America thirty or forty years ago. Today, however, soy is known far and wide — and for many good reasons! Not only does it have an exceptional nutritional content, it also contains substances that make it a functional food — a food that offers health benefits over and above its contribution in protein, vitamins, and minerals. High in phytoestrogen, phytosterol, lecithin, and other substances, soybeans have been analyzed and researched throughout the world since the mid-1980s. Today, women use soy to temper menopausal symptoms, while men use soy to lower their cholesterol. Research is still going on, confirming in many cases soy's positive impact on health.

In the same way that people in the West process wheat into dry cereal, bread, pasta, and cookies, Asians have always transformed soybeans into tofu, miso, tempeh, tamari, and shoyu. But Westerners have taken up the challenge in recent years by creating a whole new range of foods based on soy protein, tofu, and roasted soybeans. Here's an overview.

The soybean

More than two thousand years ago, soybeans belonged to the Chinese food reper-toire; a millennium later, they became part of Japanese cuisine. Whether home-cooked or canned, soybeans have a higher nutrient content than all other legumes. In fact, **250 ml (1 cup) of cooked soybeans contains 30 grams of protein,** twice as much as you'd get from the same quantity of cooked chickpeas, and the same amount you'd get from 100 g (3 1/2 oz) of lean ground beef. The protein found in soybeans has recently gained points: scientific studies measuring the effectiveness of protein in human growth now give soybeans a perfect score, equal to the score for milk and eggs.

Soybeans are also an excellent source of minerals (see Table 15, p. 53). And while 250 ml (1 cup) of cooked soybeans contains more fat than the same quantity of chickpeas, it is good source of omega-3 fatty acids, which are considered an asset these days. No other legume matches the soybean on this score.

The presence of isoflavones that mimic estrogen produced by ovaries is much higher in soybeans than in other legumes, and provides health benefits unknown ten years ago (see sidebars, pp. 40 and 41).

And along with these nutritional extras, soybeans are user-friendly and fit into recipes just like any other legume. Raw soybeans need to be soaked, then cooked in water for two to three hours to reach the right consistency. You can also use canned soybeans.

Roasted soybeans

Have you ever tried roasted soybeans, also called soy nuts? You should, they are a real treat! The beans are soaked in water, then roasted in oil or dry-roasted, and sold unsalted, salted, or seasoned. The texture and taste are similar to peanuts, but the nutritional value is surprising. A small handful of roasted soybeans (30 ml or 2 tbsp) contains 5 grams of protein — as much as a small serving of yogurt. And that handful supplies twice as much protein as the same quantity of almonds, but 30 percent less fat. They're a snack worth a second look!

Soy protein isolate

Soy protein isolate, found in many foods, is extracted from soybeans, reduced into flakes, and then put through a process to remove its fat content. It is a pure and concentrated form, 90 percent of which is protein. In fact, 15 ml (1 tbsp) of soy protein isolate sold in a powdered form can contain from 5 to 20 grams of protein. Check the product label.

Soy protein isolate is found in many soy beverages and drinks, infant formulas, a wide range of new products — such as simulated meats — and many powders sold as protein or isoflavone supplements (see Table 11, p. 41).

Soy beverages

You find soy beverages, often called soy milk, just about everywhere, from natural-foods stores to supermarkets, and even convenience stores. They come in many brands and flavours, and don't necessarily contain the same ingredients, but they are all based on soybeans — the only legume from which a rich, creamy, milk-like liquid can be made.

There are two ways to manufacture soy milk: milling and pressing soybeans that have been soaked and cooked, or adding water to soy protein isolate. Some are prepared with certified organic soybeans, others are not. The resulting beverage is pasteurized before being sold on the market.

Soy milk is sold in one- and two-litre containers and in individual portions; it is available fresh, in the refrigerated section, or as a long-lasting ultra-high-temperature (UHT) product. It is offered plain or in many flavours, including strawberry, vanilla, chocolate, and one called "original." You can use this beverage like cow's milk on breakfast cereals or in soups, sauces, sherbets, and other dishes.

The protein content varies depending on how much soy is in the product. Some beverages contain up to 9 grams of protein per 250 ml (1 cup), while others have only 5 grams. Don't confuse soy beverages with other drinks prepared with rice, almonds, or a grain base; such drinks contain little protein and much more sugar.

The calcium and vitamin D content of soy beverages depends on whether the beverage is enriched or not. An enriched soy beverage contains an average of 300 mg of calcium and 200 international units of vitamin D per 250 ml (1 cup), while a non-enriched beverage contains only 20 mg of calcium and no vitamin D at all. Enriched soy beverages also contain vitamin B_{12} — 50 percent of the daily requirement per 250 ml (1 cup) — which is the only vitamin totally absent in plant foods. Always read the labels.

Note: These beverages, even the enriched ones, are not appropriate for infants and should not be served to toddlers under two years of age. On the other hand, soy-based infant formulas are appropriate for babies and are available on the market.

Soy flour

Soy flour is made from ground roasted soybeans. It contains two to three times as much protein as whole-wheat flour, lots of iron, and many other minerals. It can be used in small quantities in baked products, but a dough made with it won't rise because it lacks gluten, the leavening agent in wheat flour. If you buy full-fat soy flour you must keep it in the refrigerator, as it rapidly turns rancid; on the other hand, the fat-free or defatted variety can be kept in the pantry without any problem.

Tempeh

We have Indonesia to thank for developing tempeh, which is a firm, chewy cake made from whole fermented soybeans. Modern tempeh is made by combining fermented soybeans with another grain, such as brown rice or millet. To prepare it, soybeans are soaked overnight in water and cooked; the mixture is then "inoculated" and left to ferment for about thirty-six hours at 30°C. The resulting product must be cooked before it can be eaten. It has a tender, chewy texture and tastes a little like mushrooms. It has more flavour when marinated for at least twenty minutes.

You can use tempeh as your main course or instead of meat or a legume in spaghetti sauce, soups, or cooked dishes. It keeps for several months in the freezer, but once thawed, it must be refrigerated and used within ten days. Tempeh contains as much protein as the same amount of cooked soybeans; 125 ml (1/2 cup) of tempeh contains 77 mg of calcium, the same as cottage cheese. Don't confuse tempeh with seitan, made with wheat gluten and not as rich in protein (see p. 16).

Simulated meats

Chicken- and beef-flavoured soy burgers, soy-based wieners, and simulated smoked meats are surprisingly "real" tasting. Try them in a meal, and your whole family will think they're eating meat.

These new foods are made with soy proteins mixed with other ingredients, such as water, wheat gluten, yeast extracts, and spices. They are usually found in the refrigerator section at the supermarket or natural-foods store — and they can be great helpers when you're in a rush.

6. COMPARATIVE VALUES OF MEAT AND SIMULATED MEAT				
Product	Quantity (g)	Energy (cal)	Protein (g)	Fat (g)
Lean ground beef, cooked	55	136	16	8
Yves Veggie Cuisine ground-meat substitute	55	58	10	0
Pepperoni	48	239	10	21
Yves Veggie Cuisine pepperoni	48	73	14	0

Soy sauce

Soy sauce is made with fermented soybeans. Once fermented, the beans are ground, boiled, filtered, then salted. There are various kinds of soy sauce:

- **Tamari** (the Japanese name for soy sauce) is made mainly of soybeans, but it may contain wheat, while **shoyu** sauce is a soy sauce that always contains wheat.
- **Teriyaki** sauce is a soy sauce to which sugar, vinegar, and spices have been added.
- **HVP** sauce is based on hydrolyzed vegetable protein that may come from soybeans, corn, or wheat. It is not fermented, but corn syrup, caramel, and salt are added to give it flavour and colour.

All of these soy sauces are highly salted; the light versions contain less salt. They add to the flavour of Asian dishes, but, unlike most soy products, they contain no protein and no isoflavones.

7. SODIUM (SALT) CONTENT IN SELECTED SOY PRODUCTS	
One portion is 15 ml (1 tbsp). Values are given in milligrams.	
Soy sauce, HVP type	1,044
Tamari sauce	933
Shoyu	841
Light tamari sauce	700
Teriyaki sauce	700
Miso	410

Miso

Miso is a fermented paste made from soybeans. There are two types of miso: hatcho-miso, made only with soybeans and fermented for three years; and miso-mamé, the more common version, made with rice or barley and fermented six to twelve months. The flavour, texture, and colour of miso vary, depending on how long it is fermented.

Miso is a substitute for salt or soy sauce, and it is high in sodium. Hatcho-miso provides some protein and isoflavones, but it is really just a seasoning. It can be added to soups, tofu, sauces, and main dishes. It keeps in the refrigerator for several months in an airtight container.

Simulated cheeses

Many of these cheeses are made with a mixture of soy proteins, water, casein, soya oil, natural flavours, salt, and various natural additives. They generally come in two forms: a firm cheese and the very popular cheese slices. Simulated cheeses are available in a variety of flavours — Quebec, Swiss, Italian, and jalapeño Jack, among others — and they contain about 4 grams of protein and 2 grams of fat per slice. You can use them just like cheese, and you can even cook with them.

8. COMPARATIVE VALUES OF CHEESE AND SIMULATED CHEESE

Portion is one slice, 17 to 20 grams.

Food	Calories	Protein (g)	Fat (g)	Calcium (mg)
Processed cheese	47	5	3	123
Soy simulated cheese	31	4	2	100

Soy yogurt

Soy yogurt is made with soybeans and water, along with tapioca and other starches, honey, fruit juices, and active bacteria: acidophilus and bifidus. It does not contain as much protein or calcium as ordinary yogurt but it is useful for people with a lactose intolerance and for strict vegetarians because of its active bacteria content.

Soy frozen desserts

Soy frozen desserts are the sweet alternative to ice cream for people who are lactose intolerant. They come in a variety of flavours and are made with soymilk, tofu, soy oil, or soy protein. But don't forget — they contain just as much sugar as real ice cream!

9. COMPARATIVE VALUES OF FROZEN DESSERTS

Portion given is 100 ml (3 1/2 oz).

Food	Calories	Protein (g)	Fat (g)	Calcium (mg)
Laura Secord ice cream	243	4	14	24
Toffuti chocolate frozen dessert	167	2	9	18

Soy puddings

Soy-based puddings, made with soy beverages, are now available in a number of flavours and have a creamy texture.

10. COMPARATIVE VALUES OF PUDDINGS

Portion given is one container.

Food	Calories	Protein (g)	Fat (g)	Calcium (mg)
Jell-O chocolate pudding	123	4	4	22
Belsoy soy-based chocolate pudding	117	4	2	21

Soybean sprouts

Soy sprouts are obtained by germinating whole soybeans, a process that takes four to seven days. The sprouts can be eaten raw or cooked. They have a much lower nutritional content than cooked soybeans or any other legume.

A bowl of soybean sprouts contains a bit more niacin and vitamin C (8 mg, compared to 3 mg) than the same amount of cooked soybeans, but that's the only plus.

In fact, compared to cooked soybeans, soybean sprouts contain less vitamin A, thiamin, and folic acid, 10 times less riboflavin (vitamin B_2), 4 times less vitamin B_6, 3 times less calcium, 7.5 times less iron, 2 times less zinc, and 2.5 times less magnesium and potassium.

In terms of protein, a bowl of soybean sprouts cannot replace a serving of meat, while a bowl of cooked soybeans can easily do the job.

Isoflavones, or soy phytoestrogens

Soy contains a number of interesting components, including isoflavones, also called phytoestrogens because they resemble human estrogen in their structure, though not their behaviour. Phytoestrogens are inactive in food but are activated in the gut by intestinal bacteria; they become much less active when the intestinal flora are affected by antibiotics, laxatives, or other intestinal conditions. Normally, isoflavones pass into the blood thirty minutes after soy has been ingested, and 10 percent are eliminated in the urine five hours after being absorbed. These isoflavones work at a strength that is one hundred to one thousand times less than that of human estrogen, but they can still make a contribution.

Soybeans and soy protein isolate contain large amounts of isoflavones. Tofu, soy beverages, and all other soy products have lesser amounts. A great deal of scientific research has been published on isoflavones since the early 1990s. Some studies have been conducted in labs, while others were clinical trials on humans. Teams of researchers from several countries have noted that isoflavones can temper menopausal symptoms, help protect the heart, improve bone density, and help prevent certain cancers (see "Vegetarianism and heart disease" and "Vegetarianism and cancer," pp. 143 and 154).

An important fact: Most studies on isoflavones have been conducted using soy protein isolate or soy products, and many researchers suspect that isoflavones work in concert with other components present in soy. Very few studies have been conducted with the isoflavone extracts now sold as pills or supplements.

ii. ISOFLAVONE CONTENT IN SELECTED SOY PRODUCTS

Values are given in milligrams.

Food	Portion	Isoflavones
Full-fat soy flour	125 ml (1/2 cup)	84
Fat-free soy flour	125 ml (1/2 cup)	64
Cooked tempeh	100 g (3 1/2 oz)	50
Cooked soybeans	50 g (2 oz)	49
Roasted soybeans	30 g (4 tbsp)	35
Soybean chips	50 g (2 oz)	32
Silken tofu, firm	100 g (3 1/2 oz)	27–29
Tempeh burger	100 g (3 1/2 oz)	26
Soy yogurt	175 g (3/4 cup)	26
Soy beverage	250 ml (1 cup)	20–35
Regular tofu	100 g (3 1/2 oz)	21
Breakfast cereal with soy (Vive)	160 ml (2/3 cup)	14
Soy protein isolate	15 ml (1 tbsp)	11
Miso	5 ml (1 tsp)	5
Soy or tamari sauce	5 ml (1 tsp)	–
Soy oil	5 ml (1 tsp)	–

Isoflavones and labels: A need for clarification

You're choosing a soy beverage. As you read different labels, you find one product that contains 70 mg of isoflavones per 250 ml (1 cup). You are surprised, because the other soy milks usually contain between 20 and 35 mg of isoflavones. Is this beverage a better buy? We're not so sure. In October 2000, we had five samples of a soy beverage claiming a content of 70 mg of isoflavones per 250 ml (1 cup) analyzed by the Guelph Centre for Functional Foods at the University of Guelph. The results revealed a content of only 33 mg of isoflavones — much less than was indicated on the label. Was this an error or a fraud? We don't know.

But we do know what a label should indicate when it comes to isoflavones. A food that contains 100 mg of total or conjugated isoflavones yields only 60 mg of active isoflavones in the form of aglycones. You can compare this to a calcium supplement that advertises a total of 1,000 mg of calcium carbonate but contains only 400 mg of elemental calcium. So, look for a label that provides the content of isoflavones in the form of aglycones, but don't trust products that claim a much higher isoflavone content than that indicated in Table 11 on p. 41. Unfortunately, few labels supply this type of information today, but this will come, as it has for elemental calcium.

Is soy a GM food?

According to Canadian regulations, soy is one of the plants that can be genetically modified (GM). Genetic modification, a new application of biotechnology, transfers genes from one species to another in order to change a plant's behaviour, to increase its resistance to certain insects, herbicides, or diseases, to retard the ripening process, and so on. At first glance, this technology seems miraculous, but it has not been *time-tested*, since the first successful genetic manipulation dates back only to 1990. That is why this practice is raising questions in the scientific community and anxiety among consumers. "These foods, most of them designed for resistance to pesticides, are missing the target," according to Gilles Éric Séralini, professor of molecular biology at Université de Caen in France and president of CRII-GEN (Comité de recherche et d'information indépendantes sur le génie génétique, or Committee for Independent Research and Information on Genetic Engineering).

The Royal Society of Canada released a report on biotechnology in February 2001. The authors of this report recommended that the evaluation process for such foods become more open and the data more widely available. These top-notch experts asked for stricter regulations, or at least a moratorium to allow time for an in-depth analysis of the scientific data and clear evidence that genetically modified foods do not have negative effects on human health. The Farmers' Association also requested a moratorium, in order to avoid heavy economic losses due to rejection of these products in markets such as that of the European Community. And consumers requested mandatory labelling. The government did set up a committee on voluntary labelling, but voted against mandatory labelling in the fall of 2001.

The situation is complex, but it isn't a lost cause. Not all plants that can be genetically modified (corn, canola, soybean, gourd, flax, potato, and tomato) are. In fact, total production of GM plants fell by at least 20 percent in the late 1990s, and only 30 percent of soybeans produced in Canada are genetically modified. Not only that, the soy used to prepare beverages, tofu, protein powders, and other products is not necessarily genetically modified. Soy is never genetically modified when it is certified organic by an accredited agency — CAQ, OCIA, Garanti BIO, Québec Vrai, FVO, OGBA, QAI Inc. — or when the label clearly states that there has been no genetic modification.

12. SOY-BASED AND TOFU PRODUCTS THAT ARE NOT GM

Alegria — Soy fettuccini, macaroni, and spaghetti
Amy's — Tofu lasagna
Eden Foods — Black soybeans (canned)
Eden Foods (soy beverage) — Edensoy carob, original, and vanilla; Edensoy
  Extra; Eden Blend (rice and soybeans)
Genisoy — Roasted soya nuts
Green Cuisine — Tempeh
Koyo — Wheat-free organic tamari; organic Japanese
La Soyarie — Regular and herb-flavoured tofu
Momo's Veggie Kitchen — Burgers
Nature's Path (cereals) — Soy Plus Granola; Optimum
Provamel — Chocolate, mocha, and hazelnut pudding; organic soy beverage:
  almond, grains, chocolate, enriched, vanilla, and sugar-free
Seapoint Farm — Edamame soybean rice bowls
Second Nature — Burgers
Soleil d'or — Soy oil
So Nice (soy beverage) — Natural, original, vanilla, chocolate, and mocha
SoSoya — Roasted soybeans
Soyaganic — Baked tofu with sauces
Soy Delicious — Organic frozen desserts
So Yummi (mousse) — Chocolate, coconut-banana, lime, raspberry
Sunrise (silken tofu) — Firm, extra-firm, and soft tofu; herb-flavoured tofu;
  tofu dessert; almond dessert

Tofu Rella — Simulated cheeses
Trés Tofu — Simulated cheeses
Turtle Island Foods — Turkey roast
Yu — Soy multigrain beverage
Yves Veggie Cuisine — Simulated meats
Yves Veggie Cuisine — Simulated cheese, sliced, in Quebec, Swiss, Italian, and jalapeño Jack flavours

5

Tofu: Try It,
You'll Like It!

Although tofu became quite popular in the 1990s, many people still haven't heard of it, while others hesitate to try it. We can't deny that tofu has an image problem, but we have to admit our weakness for it because of its superb nutrient content and its great culinary versatility.

The two types of tofu

Regular or cotton tofu looks like a fairly firm cheese. It is made with soybeans, which are cooked and then ground. The milk extracted from this process is coagulated with calcium or magnesium salts, and the resulting product is strained and pressed in a mould. The firmness of the tofu depends on how much it is pressed. The texture is spongy and granular. You buy it in blocks, fresh or vacuum-packed, ready to eat or to be used in a recipe.

A portion of 100 g (3 1/2 oz) of regular tofu contains 15 grams of protein, or as much as 250 ml (1 cup) of cooked legumes or 125 ml (1/2 cup) of cooked soybeans. When the tofu is prepared with calcium sulfate, it supplies as much calcium as two glasses of milk. It also contains 5 mg of iron, or twice as much as 100 g (3 1/2 oz) of lean ground beef. What more can we say?

Silken, or Japanese-style, tofu is totally different from regular tofu in terms of how it is made, its texture, and its composition. It is prepared with a thicker soy milk, to which lactone has been added, and a coagulant. Lactone makes the tofu firm, and so the draining and pressing stages are not necessary. Soft and white, it melts in the mouth like a firm yogurt or a custard. Because of its smooth texture, it can be used in recipes such as fruit mousse, milkshakes, or smoothies and sauces. A 170 g (6 oz) portion supplies 13 grams of protein, or almost as much as 125 ml (1/2 cup) of cooked soybeans. It contains less calcium and iron than regular tofu, but more isoflavones (see Table 11, p. 41).

How to buy and store tofu

Unpackaged **fresh tofu** is still the top choice! This is the tastiest of the regular tofus — and the most perishable. In Japan, it is used the same day it is purchased. You will generally find it stored in a tub of cold water in the refrigerator section of natural-foods stores and Asian grocery stores, and it is sold by weight. You can keep it in the refrigerator in a covered container filled with water. If you use it within twenty-four hours, you don't need to change the water in the container, but if you keep it longer, you should change the water every day and keep the container firmly closed. This type of tofu can be kept up to ten days. You can check whether tofu is fresh by smelling it: fresh tofu has a subtle, slightly sweet odour with a hint of nuts, while tofu that is past its prime has an unpleasant sour odour.

Vacuum-packed regular tofu is the most popular format available today. You can usually find it in a 454 g (1 lb) package in the refrigerator sections of supermarkets and natural-foods stores. The label has an expiration date. In general, this tofu can be kept in the package for several weeks. When you open the package, drain the water, put the tofu in a container, cover it with cold water, and cover the container. It can be kept in the refrigerator this way for up to one week.

You can firm up tofu that seems less fresh by simmering it for 3 to 5 minutes in salt water. Use 1.5 litres (6 cups) of water and 5 ml (1 tsp) of salt. Then drain the tofu on paper or a towel for 30 minutes.

You can freeze tofu, but its appearance and texture will suffer, since freezing accentuates its spongy, granular quality. Thaw it by steaming it in its package.

Silken tofu can be **soft, firm**, or **extra-firm**, and it is sold in two forms:

- In an aseptic cardboard wrapping with an expiration date. Packaged this way it lasts six months or more and doesn't need to be refrigerated as long as it has not been opened. When it is opened, you can keep it in the refrigerator in its closed package for two to three days. You'll most likely find this tofu in natural-foods stores, but today more and more supermarkets carry it.
- In a sealed package with an expiration date. This version is found in the refrigerator sections of supermarkets and natural-foods stores. The expiration date usually indicates that it can be kept for a few weeks, similar to yogurt. Once you open the package, drain the tofu and keep it in the refrigerator for two to three days.

Silken tofu is ideal in sauces, dips, puddings, shakes, smoothies, spreads, and casseroles. Of all the different types of tofu, it is the easiest to camouflage, and it is the most user-friendly tofu to start cooking with.

Fried tofu, also called *age*, is a variation on regular tofu that can be found in Asian supermarkets. It comes in packages containing twelve pieces and is sold refrigerated or frozen. It is golden in colour and spongy in texture, and has a stronger flavour. Before you add it to recipes, cut it into strips and blanch it to remove the oil it was fried in. You can keep this type of tofu in the refrigerator in its packaging without adding water.

The perfect partners

Garlic, ginger, scallions, tamari or soy sauce, rice or cider vinegar, molasses, and sesame oil are perfect partners that can liven up tofu, which might be rather plain all by itself. Use these partners to make a marinade or add them in your cooking.

Here's a very simple, all-purpose **tofu marinade** that adds a spicy aroma to tofu cubes or slices: 125 ml (1/2 cup) light tamari sauce, 30 ml (2 tbsp) each sesame oil and rice or cider vinegar, 15 ml (1 tbsp) fresh ginger, minced, and one garlic clove, chopped. Marinate the tofu for 20 to 30 minutes for added colour and taste.

The many uses of tofu

Regular fresh or packaged tofus work well in soups, cooked dishes, wok sautéed dishes, and grilled dishes. (You'll find it in many of the recipes in this book.)

Silken tofu can also be used in various ways. For example, whip in a blender half a block of soft silken tofu with a few teaspoons of plain yogurt and 15 ml (1 tbsp) of extra-virgin olive oil, some lemon zest, 15 ml (1 tbsp) of lemon juice, dill or tarragon, and two chopped garlic cloves. You'll have a tasty **creamy sauce** for grilled or poached salmon.

Tofu-based mayonnaise is easy to make, and you'll improve the quality of fat in your menu. One day, LD played a trick on her daughter, who was a bit too fond of mayonnaise. She replaced the mayonnaise in the jar with a tofu mayonnaise, and her daughter didn't notice the difference! It's a snap to make: in the food processor or the blender, blend until smooth half a block of firm silken tofu, 30 ml (2 tbsp) each of lemon juice and extra-virgin olive oil, 10 ml (2 tsp) of Dijon mustard, 5 ml (1 tsp) of honey, and salt and pepper to taste. Refrigerated, it will keep for several weeks. Not only does this mayonnaise taste great, it's also low in fat: 15 ml (1 tbsp) of tofu mayonnaise contains only 2 grams of fat, while the same quantity of ordinary commercial mayonnaise hides 11 grams.

In a muffin recipe, replace one egg with 60 ml (1/4 cup) of whipped silken tofu. You won't taste any difference.

Everyone loves the **tofu spread** that LD prepares in her course on healthy fine cuisine. It is made with one-third of a block of firm silken tofu, 30 ml (2 tbsp) sesame butter (tahini), 10 ml (2 tsp) natural peanut butter, and 5 to 10 ml (1 to 2 tsp) maple syrup, all whipped in the food processor. It's simply delicious on whole-wheat raisin bread.

6

Legumes 101: The Basics

In North America, many people are still in the dark when it comes to legumes, the star ingredients in a meatless diet. Although we use them in a few popular meals, like baked beans and pea soup, our repertoire of mainstream legume recipes pretty much ends there.

Nevertheless, you probably eat more legumes than you realize, especially if you enjoy trying foods from different cultures. Think of Italian minestrone, French lentil salad, hummus and roasted chickpeas from Lebanon, Mexican red beans, Brazilian black-bean soup, chickpea couscous from Morocco . . . the list is long, and delicious!

It's to your advantage to use legumes more often, since they have everything it takes to replace meat. With them, you can adopt an almost completely vegetarian menu without worrying about nutritional deficiencies.

What exactly are legumes?

Legumes, also called beans or pulse, are a large family of about six hundred plant foods divided into four categories: haricots or beans, soy, lentils, and peanuts. Like the summer-fresh green peas that you buy at the market, legumes grow in a pod. But unlike green peas, legumes are rarely eaten fresh. They're usually sold dry, can be stored for a long time, require soaking before cooking, and take a long time to cook. They aren't "fast food," unless you use them canned. On the other hand, their nutritional value is amazing!

The most common varieties of legumes include:

- Haricots or beans: white (baked beans), black, kidney, romano, cannellini, navy and pinto beans; black-eyed peas; mung and adzuki beans; and lupini, broad beans, and flageolets.
- Lentils: green and brown lentils, small French du Puy lentils, and red lentils (which cook in fifteen minutes).
- Peas: the best known are those used in soups. There are also garbanzo beans or chickpeas, yellow and green split peas, and pigeon peas.
- Soybeans: they're in a category all their own, and they're very versatile. They can be found fresh in their pods and in a frozen state as *edamame*, but they're usually used in their dried state. Tofu, soy beverages, and many other soy-based products come from soybeans.

The nutritional content of legumes
A good source of protein

You can eat a meatless meal without worry as long as you incorporate enough protein, since — and this is an important point — *a meal without protein cannot be considered a "real" meal.*

Legumes contain more protein than all other plant foods — enough to replace meat. In fact, **250 ml (1 cup) of cooked legumes contains as much protein as 60 g (2 oz) of meat, poultry, or fish,** and three to four times more protein than a bowl of dry cereal or brown rice or pasta.

Let's compare legumes to those vegetables known for their high protein content: 250 ml (1 cup) of cooked legumes contains three times more protein than the same amount of broccoli or baked potatoes, and twice as much as green peas or lima beans.

You might think that legumes sold as bean sprouts provide a lot of protein — but you'd be mistaken. As the beans germinate, their water content rises and the protein is diluted. For example, 250 ml (1 cup) of cooked mung beans contains 18 grams of protein, while the same quantity of mung-bean sprouts contains only 3 grams.

Soybeans contain more protein than all other legumes. Because they are so special, we've dedicated an entire chapter to the subject (see p. 33).

Low fat content

Everyone is concerned about fat — and for good reason. We generally eat too much of it. Legumes are naturally very low in fat and, like most plant foods, have absolutely no cholesterol.

Let's compare, for example, the fat content of cooked legumes to that of a small portion of meat: 250 ml (1 cup) of cooked legumes (lentils, white or red kidney beans) contains only 1 gram of fat, compared to 13 grams in a small portion of "lean" ground beef, and 11 grams in a 45 g (1 1/2 oz) portion of ordinary hard cheese.

And that's not all. It's important to remember that there are different kinds of fat, and some are less useful than others. The fat contained in ground beef and hard cheese is saturated and can raise the level of blood cholesterol, while the fat in legumes is unsaturated and helps to lower the cholesterol level.

13. FAT CONTENT OF LEGUMES

The amount given is a cooked portion of 250 ml (1 cup).
Values are given in grams.

Food	Total fat	Monounsaturated	Polyunsaturated	Saturated
Soybeans	16	3.6	9.2	2.4
Chickpeas	4	1.0	2.0	0.5
Pinto beans	1	0.2	0.3	0.2
Split peas	1	0.2	0.3	0.1
Black-eyed peas	1	0.1	0.6	0.3
Mung beans	1	0.1	0.5	0.5
Red kidney beans	1	0.1	0.4	0.1
Brown or green lentils	1	0.1	0.4	0.1
Black beans	1	0.1	0.4	0.3
White beans	1	0.1	0.3	0.2
Lima beans	1	0.04	0.4	0.2

14. FAT CONTENT OF ANIMAL FOODS

The amount given is a portion of 90 g (3 oz).
Values are given in grams.

Food	Total fat	Monounsaturated	Polyunsaturated	Saturated
Cheddar cheese	30	8.5	0.8	19.0
Mozzarella cheese	25	7.0	0.8	15.6
Camembert cheese	22	6.3	0.6	13.7
Lean ground beef, cooked	13	5.6	0.5	5.1
Chicken thigh, without skin, cooked	8	2.7	1.8	2.1
Stewing veal, cooked	4	1.3	0.4	1.2
Pork liver, cooked	4	0.6	0.9	1.3

A wealth of minerals

To various degrees, legumes are mineral storehouses. They contain appreciable amounts of iron, magnesium, zinc, potassium, calcium, manganese, and copper. In this sense, they rival meat, which also supplies a large amount of minerals.

When it comes to **iron**, 250 ml (1 cup) of cooked legumes supplies 5 to 8 milligrams of iron, as much as a portion of veal liver — famous for its high iron content — and three times as much as a portion of beef. To absorb the iron in plant protein, however, you must eat a fruit or vegetable with a high vitamin C content in the same meal (see p. 20).

Magnesium is a mineral that is extremely important in muscle relaxation. In this respect, legumes are winners: 250 ml (1 cup) of cooked legumes provides an average of 200 milligrams of magnesium, as much as a bowl of bran cereal or 80 ml (1/3 cup) of wheat germ — two foods known for their high magnesium content.

Zinc is an element essential to growth, and it is vital to the body's natural healing process. Legumes contain a good quantity of zinc: 250 ml (1 cup) of cooked legumes contains twice as much zinc as a portion of chicken or sardines.

Legumes are also an excellent source of **potassium**, an element that is crucial for maintaining normal blood pressure. In fact, 250 ml (1 cup) of cooked legumes contains an average of 700 milligrams of potassium, as much as half a banana, more than two oranges, and as much as a bowl of prunes — all foods known for their high potassium content.

15. MINERAL CONTENT OF LEGUMES

The amount given is a cooked portion of 250 ml (1 cup).
Values are given in milligrams.

Food	Calcium	Magnesium	Potassium	Iron	Zinc
Black-eyed peas	51	71	436	4	2
Soybeans	185	156	936	9	2
White beans	202	141	1,257	8	3
Lima beans	73	89	705	4	2
Mung means	53	63	231	2	1
Black beans	49	127	645	4	2
Pinto beans	87	99	846	5	2
Red kidney beans	123	90	784	6	2
Green or brown lentils	40	75	772	7	3
Split peas	29	75	750	3	2
Chickpeas	81	74	436	5	3

An important source of fibre

Only plant foods contain fibre, which makes you feel full, helps prevent constipation, and can even lower your cholesterol level. Legumes are winners here, too: 250 ml (1 cup) of cooked legumes contains between 6 and 10 grams of fibre, or as much as two raw unpeeled apples, two bowls of fresh strawberries, or 4 or 5 slices of whole-grain bread.

16. FIBRE CONTENT OF SELECTED PLANT FOODS, INCLUDING LEGUMES

The amount given is a cooked portion of 250 ml (1 cup).
Values are given in grams.

Food	Total fibre	Insoluble fibre	Soluble fibre
Legumes			
Red kidney beans	17	11	6
Black-eyed peas	17	5	12
Lima beans	14	7	7
Black beans	13	8	5
White beans	13	7	6
Broad beans	11	9	2
Green or brown lentils	9	8	1
Chickpeas	8	6	2
Split peas	6	5	1
Vegetables and fruits			
Peas	11	9	2
Brussels sprouts	10	3	7
Parsnips, sliced	7	5	2
Mixed vegetables	7	4	3
Raspberries	6	1	5
Fresh spinach	5	4	1
Broccoli	5	3	2
Snow peas	5	3	2
Carrots	5	2	3
Corn	4	3	1
Blueberries	4	3	1
Beets	4	2	2
Strawberries	4	2	2
Mango (1 medium)	4	2	2
Yellow or green string beans	3	2	1
Raw carrot, grated	3	1	2
Baked potato (1 medium)	3	1	2
Dates (3 or 4)	3	1	2
Banana (1 medium)	2	1	1

16. FIBRE CONTENT OF SELECTED PLANT FOODS, INCLUDING LEGUMES

The amount given is for 100 g (3 1/2 oz)
Values are given in grams.

Food	Total fibre	Insoluble fibre	Soluble fibre
Seeds and nuts			
Flaxseeds	39	19	20
Whole almonds	15	14	1
Pistachios	10.3	10	0.3
Sesame seeds	11	8	3
Hazelnuts	8.4	8	0.4
Brazil nuts or walnuts	6	5	1
Whole grains			
Wheat germ	18	14	4
Pot barley	5	3	2
Millet	4	2.5	1.5
Brown rice	2	1	1

An excellent source of folic acid

Folic acid has recently made the news since it was shown to be most useful in reducing the risk of spina bifida, a birth defect of the central nervous system, when supplied adequately in the diet before pregnancy. This vitamin has also been shown to reduce elevated levels of homocysteine, considered a risk factor for heart disease. Folic acid is often inadequate in our diet these days. But legumes, especially lentils, are one of the best sources.

In fact, 250 ml (1 cup) of cooked lentils provides 378 micrograms (mcg) of folic acid, as much as there is in a portion of veal liver, renowned for its high folic acid content.

17. FOLIC ACID CONTENT OF LEGUMES

The amount given is a cooked portion of 250 ml (1 cup).
Values are given in micrograms (mcg).

Green or brown lentils	378
Pinto beans	311
Black beans	270
White beans	269

Daily nutritional intake recommended by the National Academy of Sciences in 2001: 400 mcg.

A very low glycemic index

In addition to containing protein, vitamins, minerals, and fibre, legumes are high in carbohydrates, or starch. But unlike many other starchy foods, such as bread, rice, and potatoes, legumes have a very low glycemic index — meaning they don't cause a rapid rise of blood-sugar levels. The glycemic index concept was first developed by a team of scientists led by Dr. David Jenkins at the University of Toronto. Today, clinical studies in many countries have shown that foods with a low glycemic index help control blood-sugar levels in people with diabetes, can reduce the secretion of insulin, and even help to delay hunger pangs. Legumes have a glycemic index of between 30 and 45, while white bread and white rice have a glycemic index of 70.

Canned legumes have a glycemic index slightly higher than home-cooked legumes because of the high temperatures involved in the canning process. Nevertheless, it is still lower than that of bread, crackers, or rice.

Buying legumes

When you are buying legumes, you have to choose between dried legumes, which you have to cook, and canned legumes, which are ready to serve. Cooking legumes takes longer, but the result is delicious.

Whether you are buying dried legumes in bulk or in a package, you should always choose beans, lentils, or dried peas that are shiny, smooth, and uniform. Legumes that are too dry or broken are more friable and take longer to cook.

You'll usually find a greater variety of legumes at natural-foods stores and

Middle Eastern or Indian grocery stores than in the supermarket. If the store is a busy one, its products are usually fresh.

Canned legumes are sold in 540 ml (19 oz) and 398 ml (14 oz) tins. They can also occasionally be found in a 227 ml (8 oz) tin with a cover that does not require a can opener. These legumes are usually kept in salt water, but lately stores have begun to offer new legume salads in a marinade of olive oil, wine vinegar, lemon juice, spices, and herbs.

Storage

Dry legumes can be stored for a long time in a cool place, below $21°$C ($70°$F), in an air-tight container or a glass jar. It is better to use them within twelve months of buying them.

To soak or not to soak

Although preparing dried legumes takes a number of hours, it is very simple. Before cooking or soaking, wash the beans, lentils, or dried peas in cold water and sort them so you can throw out any broken ones, pebbles, or bits of straw that might be present.

You don't have to soak lentils or yellow and green split peas. Soaking is essential, though, for all other legumes. Not only does it reduce the cooking time, it helps you eliminate beans that are too dry — which are the ones that rise to the surface of the water.

Soaking methods

The conventional method: Use about 1 litre (4 cups) of cold water for every 250 ml (1 cup) of dried legumes. Leave to soak in a large bowl overnight or for 10 to 12 hours at room temperature. If the room is too hot, place the bowl in the refrigerator to avoid fermentation, which gives off a yeasty odour.

The quick method: Use 750 ml (3 cups) of cold water for every 250 ml (1 cup) of dried legumes. Bring to a boil in a large pot and boil 1 to 2 minutes. Remove from heat, cover, and let sit for one hour. Discard soaking water and cook. When you use this method, the legumes absorb as much water in one hour as they would overnight.

The microwave method: Use 1 litre (4 cups) of cold water for every 250 ml (1 cup) of dried legumes. Place in a large microwave-safe bowl, cover, and cook 15 minutes at high intensity, or until boiling, then let sit in the oven for one hour. Discard water and resume cooking.

Cooking

Here, too, you have several methods to choose from: you can cook legumes on the stovetop, in the oven, in a pressure cooker, or in a slow cooker (crockpot).

Whichever method you choose, you will know your legumes are cooked when they are easily mashed by a fork. Unlike crunchy vegetables or pasta al dente, the digestibility of legumes is increased when they are cooked thoroughly — and gas problems are reduced.

The size of the legume makes no difference, but higher altitude, hard water, and old beans will increase the cooking time.

For all types of cooking, except in the pressure cooker, cover the legumes with cold water, bring to a strong boil, and boil for 10 minutes. Then skim and add seasoning, such as onions, garlic, sage, and carrots, depending on the recipe. Never add salt at the beginning of cooking, because it prolongs the cooking time and slows down the softening of the beans. Instead, wait one hour, then add salt when the legumes are slightly soft. The same is true for adding acidic foods such as tomatoes, wine, vinegar, or lemon juice. (Lentils and peas are an exception; they taste better when salt is added early in the cooking.)

Cooking in a microwave oven doesn't really save time, since you have to stir the legumes every 15 minutes and change the heat intensity often.

Seasonings that add flavour

Certain condiments combine marvellously with legumes and enhance their flavour. For 250 ml (1 cup) of soaked legumes, add to the cooking water 2 bay leaves, 1 small onion cut in quarters, a few sprigs of parsley, 1 sliced garlic clove, and 5 ml (1 tsp) of extra-virgin olive oil.

The issue of flatulence or gas

The more often you eat legumes, the less gas and bloating you will have. But before you reach this state of grace, you can reduce or prevent gas by taking a few simple measures:

18. COOKING TIME OF LEGUMES

The amount given is a portion of 250 ml (1 cup).

Legumes	Soaking essential	Cooking time
Red lentils	no	20 to 35 min
Green or brown lentils	no	45 min to 1 hr
Split peas	no	45 min to 1 hr
Black-eyed peas	yes	40 min to 1 hr
Lima beans (large)	yes	1 hr, 30 min
Lima beans (small)	yes	45 min to 1 hr, 15 min
Romano beans	yes	1 hr to 1 hr, 30 min
Soybeans	yes	3 hrs
Flageolets	yes	1 hr
White beans	yes	1 hr, 30 min
Cannellini beans	yes	1 hr to 1 hr, 30 min
Mung beans	yes	1 hr to 1 hr, 30 min
Black beans	yes	1 hr, 30 min
Pinto beans	yes	1 hr to 1 hr, 30 min
Red kidney beans	yes	1 hr
Chickpeas	yes	2 hr, 30 min to 3 hrs

Note: 250 ml (1 cup) of legumes usually doubles in volume when cooked.

- Rinse the legumes before soaking them, change the soaking water two or three times during the twelve hours of soaking, and discard the soaking water before cooking.
- Cook the legumes until they can be mashed very easily with a fork.
- Put the cooked legumes in a food processor and purée them, then eat them in a soup or in a purée such as hummus.
- Start by eating small amounts of legumes, perhaps 80 ml (1/3 cup), and test your reaction. Let your body gradually get used to them by eating just one legume meal per week.
- Do not add sugar to a legume recipe, as it encourages fermentation. Think of the concert of gas that follows a meal of baked beans full of molasses!
- Avoid a sweet dessert or dried fruits at the same meal, since the mixture of legumes and sugar encourages fermentation.

- Try the enzyme alpha galactosidase, sold in pills or drops under the brand name Beano in drugstores and natural-foods stores. If you take one pill or a few drops of the enzyme before you eat legumes, you will greatly lessen the occurrence of flatulence.
- Add a bit of cumin to your recipe, or drink an infusion of cumin — 5 ml (1 tsp) of powdered cumin in 250 ml (1 cup) of hot water, infused for 5 minutes — after your legume meal. This spice has great anti-gas powers!

Storage after cooking

Cooked legumes can be kept in the refrigerator for just a few days. When you cook them yourself, think about cooking a large quantity, using what you need and freezing the rest.

Once they are cooked and cooled, you can easily freeze legumes in plastic containers or freezer bags, in small quantities of one to four servings, as needed. They keep in the freezer up to eight months.

To thaw legumes, place them in a steamer and steam them before integrating them into your recipes.

Legumes, even precooked, are a must in a meatless menu.

• • •

7

The 25 Menus
and Their Recipes

A part-time vegetarian diet translates into a new set of winning menus. You can alternate among tasty fish or seafood meals, delicious lasagnas with vegetables and fresh cheeses, pasta with vegetarian sauces, flans and quiches with or without crust, omelets with herbs, and other dishes in which eggs and cheese are the main sources of protein. All these dishes fit into a healthy diet, but because there is a general lack of recipes featuring legumes and tofu, our winning menus give priority to these two pillars of a nutritious vegetarian diet.

Our twenty-five menus are designed to take various factors into account:

- **Simplicity**. The meals don't have elaborate appetizers or fancy trimmings. The main dish is accompanied by a luscious salad or some cooked vegetable, and the dessert is most often a fresh fruit, served plain or dressed up a little.
- **Quick preparation**. The ingredients are either easy to find or can conveniently be replaced with our suggested substitutes. Almost every menu can be prepared in the wink of an eye. They are designed for people who don't have time to cook fancy meals every night.

- **New flavours**. New ingredients such as tofu, black-eyed peas, cumin, and bok-choy will become user-friendly. And because flavour is a must from start to finish, we make use of many spices and fresh herbs. We have also put together appetizing combinations using foods that don't sound all that exciting on their own.
- **Health**. Eating smart is the cornerstone of our approach! The stars on our menus are legumes, tofu, beautiful vegetables, whole grains, and ripe and juicy fruits — the updated version of a healthier menu.

All the meatless dishes contain a minimum of 15 grams of protein per serving, as required. And each complete menu contains sufficient vitamin C to improve iron absorption, as long as the suggested vegetable or fruit is served.

How many soy or legume meals can one eat per week?

The secret of a healthy diet is to eat many different foods on a regular basis. Soy and legumes come in many different shapes and flavours; they can help you reduce your meat intake, but they also enrich your recipe file.

If you wish to do so, you may eat soy every day, in dishes prepared with soybeans, tofu, or soy beverages. The same goes for legumes. These foods supply good protein and some iron, two nutrients that must be watched closely, especially if you have taken meat out of your diet completely. But remember our advice: if these foods are new to you, do not overdo it: go slowly at first to avoid gas problems.

Some friendly advice

When you serve a meal featuring legumes or tofu,

- Be assertive! Serve the dish without advertising the main ingredients, since some people resist change. Make sure the dish is well seasoned, present it well, add colourful vegetables, and don't make a big deal about it.
- If you're just starting with vegetarian cooking, begin by serving simple dishes on weeknights before undertaking a meatless feast.
- If you want to serve a vegetarian dish for a dinner party, try the crêpe gateau (p. 80) — you'll be thrilled with the response you get. This dish is impressive and tastes delicious, and everyone will want the recipe.

- For other good ideas for meatless meals, see the section "Some Good Resources for Your Kitchen Library," p. 195.

> I'm lucky to have vegetarian friends who allow me to try new meatless recipes when they come over. For these dinners, I choose vegetarian recipes that are more elaborate than those I prepare on ordinary weeknights.
> LLL

The types of tofu used in our recipes:
- **Silken** tofu, which is also called Japanese-style tofu. This tofu has a fine texture and can be easily creamed. It is found in three forms — soft, firm, and extra-firm — in natural-foods stores and some supermarkets and grocery stores. The most common brands are Mori-Nu, Kikkoman, and Sunrise.
- **Regular** tofu, which is also called cotton tofu. This tofu has a more granular texture and is sold in the refrigerator sections of all supermarkets. The most common brands are La Soyarie, Nutrisoya, and Unisoya.

About legumes:
- When legumes are included in recipes, you can use home-cooked legumes or canned legumes.
- Lentils do not require soaking and cook quite rapidly. They are tastier when home-cooked.

Menu 1

**Prepared in less than 20 minutes,
and filled with nutrients**

Savory white beans with mushrooms

Green salad with olive oil vinaigrette

Rye bread

Orange slices with strawberry coulis*

* See recipe for raspberry coulis on p. 133 and substitute strawberries.

Savory white beans with mushrooms

Makes 3 servings

2 garlic cloves, crushed

1 small onion, finely chopped

5 ml (1 tsp) dry oregano

15 ml (1 tbsp) olive oil

227 g (1/2 lb) fresh mushrooms, sliced

540 ml (19 oz) canned white beans, drained

Juice of 1 lemon

Freshly ground pepper

Fresh parsley, finely chopped

Sauté the garlic, onion, and oregano in the olive oil for 3 minutes or until the onion is transparent. Add the mushrooms and sauté until they are cooked. Add the white beans and lemon juice. Season and cook for 5 minutes to blend flavours well. Remove from heat and let cool. Serve lukewarm and garnish with fresh parsley.

NUTRITIONAL VALUE PER SERVING	
Calories	267
Protein	16 g
Total fat	5.5 g
Monounsaturated fat	3.4 g
Polyunsaturated fat	0.8 g
Saturated fat	0.8 g
Fibre	10 g
Calcium	150 mg
Iron	6.6 mg
Magnesium	101 mg
Potassium	1,146 mg
Folic acid	140 mcg
Vitamin C	19 mg

Menu 2
The tofu is well hidden;
no one will guess!
A tasty, colourful meal

Tofu and ginger pizza

Spinach, red onion, and mushroom salad

Orange-blossom cantaloupe*

* You can find orange-blossom water in
natural-foods stores and fine grocery stores.

Tofu and ginger pizza

Makes 2 servings

60 ml (1/4 cup) pizza sauce or tomato sauce

2 small pizza crusts, 20 x 20 cm (8 x 8 in), or whole-wheat pita breads

60 ml (1/4 cup) pickled ginger (sushi ginger)

24 slices of soy pepperoni

30 ml (2 tbsp) sun-dried tomatoes in oil, finely chopped

125 ml (1/2 cup) grated cheddar cheese

5 ml (1 tsp) dried basil

Preheat the oven to 190° C (375° F). Spread the pizza sauce on the two crusts or pita breads.

Spread the ginger, soy pepperoni slices, and sun-dried tomatoes on the two crusts. Garnish with grated cheese and basil. Bake for 10 minutes, and finish by putting under the broiler for 2 minutes.

NUTRITIONAL VALUE PER SERVING	
Calories	335
Protein	24 g
Total fat	12 g
Monounsaturated fat	2.5 g
Polyunsaturated fat	1 g
Saturated fat	8 g
Fibre	5 g
Calcium	254 mg
Iron	5 mg
Magnesium	65 mg
Potassium	400 mg
Folic acid	25 mcg
Vitamin C	4 mg

Variations on vegetarian pizza

Tomato sauce
Goat cheese
Fresh dill or other herb
Drizzled olive oil

Pesto
Marinated artichoke hearts
Thin slices of grilled eggplant
Mozzarella

Tomato sauce
Grilled red bell peppers
Black olives
Grated feta cheese
Capers (optional)

Salsa
Red or black beans, cooked
Old cheddar
Green onions, chopped

Pizza sauce
Small cubes of marinated tofu
   (oil, vinegar, and garlic)
Bell peppers and mushrooms
Cheese to taste

Fresh tomatoes
Red onion, finely chopped
Fresh basil
Drizzled olive oil
Parmesan

Menu 3

An inspired dish to win over people
who "can't stand" tofu

You can use regular or extra-firm silken tofu: both will work well.

Tofu triangles with honey, mustard, and miso

Brown rice with roasted almonds

Red bell pepper salad

Fresh mango

Tofu triangles with honey, mustard, and miso

Makes 4 servings

1 block of regular tofu,* 454 g (1 lb), very well drained
15 ml (1 tbsp) miso**
30 ml (2 tbsp) Dijon mustard
30 ml (2 tbsp) light tamari or light soy sauce
15 ml (1 tbsp) honey
15 ml (1 tbsp) cold-pressed sesame oil

Cut the tofu into slices of just over 1 cm (1/2 in). Then cut each slice diagonally to form triangles.

In a bowl, mix the miso, mustard, tamari or soy sauce, honey, and sesame oil with a fork until smooth. Pour this sauce into a shallow bowl and immerse the tofu triangles until well coated.

Cover a cookie sheet with aluminum foil and place the tofu triangles on it.

Place an oven rack at a setting roughly 15 cm (5 or 6 in) under the broiler element and place the cookie sheet on it. Cook under the broiler for 3 to 5 minutes, then flip the triangles and cook them on the other side until golden.

Remove from the oven and let sit a few minutes before serving.

NUTRITIONAL VALUE PER SERVING	
Calories	156
Protein	15 g
Total fat	10 g
Monounsaturated fat	2.9 g
Polyunsaturated fat	5 g
Saturated fat	1.4 g
Fibre	1.7 g
Calcium	135 mg
Iron	6 mg
Magnesium	121 mg
Potassium	177 mg
Folic acid	20 mcg
Vitamin C	—

* If you use extra-firm silken tofu, use 2 blocks of 349 g (12.3 oz). Place each block of tofu between two small cutting boards or plates and press firmly to extract as much liquid as possible. Repeat until the tofu is as dry as possible.

** If you don't have miso, increase the quantity of tamari sauce by 5 ml (1 tsp).

Menu 4

Suzanne's lentils, a new and
updated version of a
famous Lebanese dish

Wild rice is used instead of white rice.

Suzanne's lentils
Warm broccoli with orange vinaigrette dressing
Fresh pineapple boat*

*To make a boat, take a whole fresh pineapple
and cut it lengthwise into 4 or 6 sections.
Cut out the fibrous central part,
then cut into the flesh in a square pattern.

Suzanne's lentils

Makes 4 servings

125 ml (1/2 cup) wild rice

15 ml (1 tbsp) extra-virgin olive oil

1 large or 2 small onions, finely chopped

3 cloves garlic, crushed

15 ml (1 tbsp) curry powder

250 ml (1 cup) green or du Puy lentils

125 ml (1/2 cup) orzo*

1 litre (4 cups) vegetable broth

2 ml (1/2 tsp) dried thyme

Soak the wild rice in a bowl overnight at room temperature.

In a large pot, heat the oil over low heat and brown the onion and garlic. Add the curry powder, lentils, and orzo.

Drain the wild rice, then incorporate it into the curry mixture. Pour in the vegetable broth and bring to a boil. Cover and simmer over low heat for 45 minutes or until the lentils are tender but not falling apart. Add extra broth during cooking, if necessary.

Sprinkle with thyme and serve with a green salad or green vegetable.

* Orzo is a small pasta that resembles long-grain rice. If you can't find it, replace the orzo with pot barley.

NUTRITIONAL VALUE PER SERVING	
Calories	397
Protein	20 g
Total fat	6 g
Monounsaturated fat	2.7 g
Polyunsaturated fat	0.8 g
Saturated fat	0.6 g
Fibre	8 g
Calcium	49 mg
Iron	6.3 mg
Magnesium	85 mg
Potassium	670 mg
Folic acid	270 mcg
Vitamin C	5 mg

Menu 5
A tasty Mediterranean-style meal
made in a flash

Minute minestrone with chickpeas

Whole-grain bread

Crispy salad of red and green bell peppers

Strawberry cream

Minute minestrone with chickpeas

Makes 4 servings

15 ml (1 tbsp) olive oil

1 onion, chopped

15 ml (1 tbsp) garlic, finely chopped

1 tomato, chopped

15 ml (1 tbsp) tomato paste

500 ml (2 cups) chickpeas,* cooked or canned

750 ml (3 cups) vegetable broth

180 ml (3/4 cup) small whole-wheat pasta

10 ml (2 tsp) dried basil

5 ml (1 tsp) dried oregano

60 ml (1/4 cup) fresh parsley, chopped

Salt and pepper to taste

60 ml (1/4 cup) fresh Parmesan, grated

In a pot, heat the oil over low heat and brown the onion and garlic for 3 minutes or until the onion is transparent. Add the tomato and tomato paste, stirring constantly, and cook for one minute.

NUTRITIONAL VALUE PER SERVING	
Calories	297
Protein	15 g
Total fat	8.6 g
Monounsaturated fat	3.6 g
Polyunsaturated fat	1.5 g
Saturated fat	1.8 g
Fibre	7 g
Calcium	159 mg
Iron	4 mg
Magnesium	72 mg
Potassium	472 mg
Folic acid	166 mcg
Vitamin C	15 mg

Add the chickpeas and broth. Bring to a boil and add the pasta, basil, and oregano. Reduce heat and simmer uncovered for 10 to 15 minutes or until the pasta is al dente.

Add the fresh parsley, season to taste, and garnish each serving with Parmesan.

Variation: Add 5 ml (1 tsp) of pesto, if desired.

* You can replace the chickpeas with any other cooked legume.

Strawberry cream

Makes 4 servings

375 ml (1 1/2 cup) soft silken tofu

5 ml (1 tsp) vanilla

500 ml (2 cups) ripe strawberries
or 300 g (10 oz) frozen strawberries, thawed

5 ml (1 tsp) lemon zest

15 ml (1 tbsp) honey

Put all ingredients in the blender or food processor. Mix until it is smooth and creamy. Serve cold.

NUTRITIONAL VALUE PER SERVING	
Calories	96
Protein	6 g
Total fat	2.3 g
Monounsaturated fat	0.5 g
Polyunsaturated fat	1.5 g
Saturated fat	—
Fibre	1 g
Calcium	186 mg
Iron	1.6 mg
Magnesium	88 mg
Potassium	276 mg
Folic acid	37 mcg
Vitamin C	31 mg

Menu 6

Just reading this recipe for
Moroccan-style tofu and 5-Jewel
couscous makes your mouth water!

This menu, served with greens and citrus fruits,
is overflowing with antioxidants.

Moroccan-style tofu and 5-jewel couscous
Steamed Swiss chard or spinach
Citrus fruit salad — orange and grapefruit

Moroccan-style tofu and 5-jewel couscous

Makes 4 servings

Moroccan-style tofu

30 ml (2 tbsp) extra-virgin olive oil

454 g (1 lb) regular firm tofu, well drained and cut into small cubes

1 onion, chopped

2 cloves garlic, finely chopped

7 ml (1 1/2 tsp) ground ginger

7 ml (1 1/2 tsp) ground cinnamon

2 ml (1/2 tsp) ground cumin

2 ml (1/2 tsp) paprika

250 ml (1 cup) vegetable broth

30 ml (2 tbsp) honey

Juice and zest of 1 lemon

5-jewel couscous

250 ml (1 cup) quick-cooking couscous

60 ml (1/4 cup) dried cranberries, chopped

60 ml (1/4 cup) dried apricots, chopped

45 ml (3 tbsp) fresh parsley, chopped

45 ml (3 tbsp) fresh mint, chopped

Salt and pepper to taste

125 ml (1/2 cup) roasted almonds, sliced

In a large pot, heat 15 ml (1 tbsp) of oil at medium-high heat and sauté the tofu for 7 minutes, until the cubes are golden. Remove the tofu from the pot and set aside.

In the same pot, heat the rest of the oil over medium heat and sauté the onion and garlic for 5 minutes. Add the ginger, cinnamon, cumin, and paprika, and cook for 1 minute. Add the tofu cubes, broth, honey, and lemon juice and zest, and bring to a boil. Reduce the heat, cover, and simmer over low heat for 15 minutes so the flavours blend.

At the same time, cook the couscous with the cranberries and apricots according to the directions on the package, and separate the grains with a fork. Incorporate the parsley and mint, then season to taste.

Serve the Moroccan-style tofu on a nest of couscous and garnish with roasted almonds.

NUTRITIONAL VALUE PER SERVING	
Calories	431
Protein	18 g
Total fat	20 g
Monounsaturated fat	10.7 g
Polyunsaturated fat	5.5 g
Saturated fat	2.5
Fibre	6 g
Calcium	336 mg
Iron	9.8 mg
Magnesium	185 mg
Potassium	528 mg
Folic acid	53 mcg
Vitamin C	13 mg

Menu 7
Here's a menu fit for a feast!

The layered crêpe gateau
is a spectacular dish,
and all your guests will
want to know the secret.
It's easy to make but requires a
long preparation well in advance.

The dish must be prepared in steps:
• First make the crêpes, then freeze them.
• The next day, make the lentil filling. It can be frozen or
kept in the refrigerator for 2 days.
• The spinach filling will keep in the refrigerator for 2 days.
• Make the mornay sauce the same day it will be served.
• You can assemble the crêpe gateau 2 hours in advance
without the sauce and keep it in the refrigerator, covered with plastic wrap.

Mediterranean-style grilled red bell peppers*

Layered crêpe gateau

Green salad with hazelnut oil dressing**

Pears poached in port

* You can find roasted red bell peppers from Bulgaria in fine grocery stores
in glass jars or you can roast them yourself. Serve with thin slices
or cubes of feta cheese for a delightful appetizer.
** You can replace hazelnut oil with walnut or sesame oil.

Layered crêpe gateau
Makes 8 servings

Crêpe batter
Makes 10 very thin crêpes, 20 cm (8 in) in diameter

250 ml (1 cup) whole-wheat pastry flour
1 ml (1/4 tsp) salt
2 eggs
30 ml (2 tbsp) cold-pressed canola oil
250 ml (1 cup) skim milk

Put all the ingredients in a blender or food processor and mix until smooth, about 2 minutes. Let sit 30 minutes.

Pour about 60 ml (1/4 cup) of the crêpe batter into a hot, lightly oiled cast-iron pan or a crêpe pan 20 cm (8 in) in diameter. Brown the crêpes on both sides, then place them on a plate with a sheet of waxed paper between each two. When you have finished cooking, cover the crêpes with aluminum foil so they don't dry out. You can keep them a few days in the refrigerator or freeze them.

NUTRITIONAL VALUE PER SERVING OF LAYERED CREPE GATEAU	
Calories	409
Protein	20 g
Total fat	17 g
Monounsaturated fat	6.5 g
Polyunsaturated fat	2.3 g
Saturated fat	6.7 g
Fibre	10 g
Calcium	285 mg
Iron	6.5 mg
Magnesium	148 mg
Potassium	1,185 mg
Folic acid	314 mcg
Vitamin C	48 mg

Red lentil and tomato filling

625 ml (2 1/2 cups) tomato juice or vegetable-cooking water

250 ml (1 cup) red lentils

1 to 2 garlic cloves, chopped

1 large onion, finely sliced

15 ml (1 tbsp) cold-pressed canola oil

398 ml (14 oz) canned tomatoes

5 ml (1 tsp) oregano

Salt and pepper to taste

In a pot, bring the tomato juice or vegetable-cooking water to a boil. Add the lentils and let simmer 10 to 12 minutes or until the liquid has evaporated and the lentils are tender. Remove from heat and set aside.

In another pot, brown the garlic and onion in the oil, then add the tomatoes with their juice. Bring to a boil and let simmer 10 to 15 minutes or until thick.

Remove from heat and add to the lentils. Season with oregano, salt, and pepper. Cover and refrigerate until assembling the gateau.

Spinach filling

2 pears, peeled and seeded

3 bags fresh spinach

15 ml (1 tbsp) butter

2 ml (1/2 tsp) nutmeg

Salt and pepper to taste

Poach the pears in a small amount of water for about 10 minutes. Drain, then mash the pears. Place the washed, dripping spinach in a large pot without adding water. Cover the pot and cook over medium heat about 7 minutes or until spinach is tender. Drain and chop fine or purée in the blender or food processor.

Add the pears, butter, and nutmeg. Mix well.

Correct the seasoning, cover, and refrigerate until assembling the gateau.

Mornay sauce

60 ml (1/4 cup) butter

90 ml (6 tbsp) whole-wheat pastry flour

375 ml (1 1/2 cups) chicken stock

250 ml (1 cup) skim milk

125 ml (1/2 cup) fresh parsley, finely chopped

90 g (3 oz) part-skim mozzarella cheese, grated

Salt and pepper to taste

Sherry (optional)

In a pot, melt the butter over low heat, then incorporate the unsifted pastry flour to make a roux.

Cook the roux briefly, then gradually add the chicken stock. Mix until thickened and then add the milk. Cook for 10 minutes, stirring.

Add the fresh parsley and 60 g (2 oz) of cheese, then let the cheese melt over low heat.

Remove from heat and season with salt, pepper, and a few drops of sherry.

Assembling the gateau

About 1 hour before the meal, preheat the oven to 190° C (375° F).

Lightly oil an oven-safe round, flat dish or a pizza plate. Place one crêpe on it and cover with about 125 ml (1/2 cup) lentil filling.

Place another crêpe, then spread about 80 ml (1/3 cup) of spinach filling.

Continue to assemble alternate layers of crêpe and filling. Finish with a crêpe.

Coat with one third of the mornay sauce, then cover with aluminum foil loosely enough that it doesn't touch the gateau.

Cook for 45 minutes, then remove the aluminum foil. Sprinkle with 30 g (1 oz) of grated mozzarella and place briefly under the broiler to brown. Let sit 5 minutes.

With a serrated knife, cut into slices (like slicing a pie) and coat each slice with mornay sauce. Serve immediately.

Pears poached in port

Makes 4 servings

8 allspice cloves

15 ml (1 tbsp) pink peppercorns

500 ml (2 cups) cranberry juice

60 ml (1/4 cup) sugar

250 ml (1 cup) tawny (or other) port

1 small stick of cinnamon

10 to 12 slices fresh peeled ginger, paper-thin

1 piece of orange zest 5 cm (2 in) long

60 ml (1/4 cup) dried cranberries

4 Bosc or Anjou pears, ripe and with stem

Place the allspice cloves and pink peppercorns in a small square of cheesecloth, then tie securely to make a small bag.

Pour the cranberry juice into a deep pot, add the bag of spices, the sugar, port, cinnamon, ginger, orange zest, and cranberries, then bring to a boil. Lower the heat and simmer, uncovered, 15 to 20 minutes.

Peel the pears, leaving the stems attached. Withdraw the bag of spices and place the pears standing in the boiling syrup, then poach them, uncovered, 20 to 30 minutes, depending on how ripe the pears are. Once cooked, remove the pears and place them on a serving dish.

Boil the syrup 10 to 15 minutes more to reduce it to about 180 ml (3/4 cup). Remove the cinnamon, orange zest, and ginger.

Pour the syrup over the pears and serve warm or cold.

If there is syrup left over, it can be kept in the refrigerator for several weeks.

NUTRITIONAL VALUE PER SERVING	
Calories	296
Protein	1 g
Total fat	—
Monounsaturated fat	—
Polyunsaturated fat	—
Saturated fat	—
Fibre	5 g
Calcium	36 mg
Iron	1 mg
Magnesium	18 mg
Potassium	362 mg
Folic acid	16 mcg
Vitamin C	54 mg

Menu 8

The spices of India and
soy of Asia combine beautifully
in this main-dish soup.

To top things off, the mango cream makes
a light and inspiring dessert.

Indian-style main-dish red lentil soup

Grilled whole-wheat pita

Green salad

Mango cream

Indian-style main-dish red lentil soup

Makes 6 servings

15 ml (1 tbsp) extra-virgin olive oil

30 ml (2 tbsp) mustard seeds

30 ml (2 tbsp) cumin seeds

30 ml (2 tbsp) fennel seeds

1 onion, finely chopped

30 ml (2 tbsp) fresh ginger, finely chopped

2 ml (1/2 tsp) hot-pepper flakes (optional)

500 ml (2 cups) vegetable broth

625 ml (2 1/2 cups) unflavoured soy beverage

796 ml (28 oz) canned tomatoes with juice, diced

250 ml (1 cup) red lentils

3 medium carrots, chopped

Salt and pepper

Fresh parsley, finely chopped

Plain yogurt (optional)

NUTRITIONAL VALUE PER SERVING	
Calories	262
Protein	17 g
Total fat	7 g
Monounsaturated fat	3.1 g
Polyunsaturated fat	1.7 g
Saturated fat	0.7 g
Fibre	10 g
Calcium	140 mg
Iron	7.2 mg
Magnesium	110 mg
Potassium	1,032 mg
Folic acid	175 mcg
Vitamin C	34 mg

In a large, thick-bottomed pot, heat the oil over medium-high heat, then add the mustard, cumin, and fennel seeds. Cover and let sizzle 15 to 30 seconds or until the mustard seeds start to bounce. Immediately turn off the heat, and let sit until the seeds stop bouncing.

Add the onion, ginger, and pepper flakes. Sauté this mixture with the seeds for 2 minutes, stirring well.

Add the vegetable broth, soy beverage, and tomatoes and bring to a boil. Reduce heat and incorporate the lentils and carrots. Cover and simmer for 20 minutes or until the lentils are cooked. Season to taste. Garnish with fresh parsley before serving.

To lighten the spicy flavour of this soup, you can serve it with plain yogurt. Let your guests add yogurt to the soup themselves.

Mango cream
Makes 6 servings

4 small yellow mangoes* or two large red-and-green mangoes, ripe
15 to 25 ml (1 to 1 1/2 tbsp) fresh ginger
349 g (12.3 oz) firm silken tofu

Peel and cut the mangoes into pieces and grate the ginger.

In the blender, blend the mangoes, ginger, and tofu until smooth.

Serve in your prettiest dessert cups.

* This dessert is especially smooth and creamy when made with small Mexican yellow mangoes.

NUTRITIONAL VALUE PER SERVING	
Calories	103
Protein	5 g
Total fat	1.8 g
Monounsaturated fat	0.5 g
Polyunsaturated fat	1 g
Saturated fat	—
Fibre	3 g
Calcium	130 mg
Iron	0.8 mg
Magnesium	65 mg
Potassium	279 mg
Folic acid	37 mcg
Vitamin C	29 mg

Menu 9

The idea for this menu came from Jacques Robert of the restaurant Au Tournant de la rivière*

This menu is easy to prepare,
but elegant enough for company.

Chickpeas au gratin

Moulded couscous**

Endive salad

Cantaloupe and strawberries with peppermint

* Au Tournant de la rivière is a wonderful restaurant located south-east of Montreal.
** Couscous, rice, bulghur, quinoa, and millet look lovely when
served in a moulded shape. Press the cooked grain into small Pyrex dishes,
then turn each portion onto a plate. Garnish with a fresh herb. This
presentation is ideal to serve a whole grain that is a little overcooked and sticky.

Chickpeas au gratin
Makes 4 servings

6 tomatoes, cut in large pieces

1 onion, chopped

5 to 6 cloves of garlic, chopped

15 ml (1 tbsp) olive oil

Saffron to taste

500 ml (2 cups) broth, chicken or vegetable

Salt and pepper to taste

2 small eggplants, sliced

2 zucchinis, sliced

1 litre (4 cups) chickpeas, cooked or canned

125 ml (1/2 cup) almonds or hazelnuts, finely chopped

Make the sauce by sautéeing the tomatoes, onion, and garlic in the olive oil. Add the saffron and broth, then season to taste.

Sauté the eggplant and zucchini slices in a pan without any oil, just to remove water.

In a casserole dish, arrange the chickpeas and the eggplant and zucchini slices in layers. Cover with the sauce and garnish with the chopped nuts.

Cook in the oven at 180° C (350° F) for 30 to 40 minutes.

NUTRITIONAL VALUE PER SERVING	
Calories	319
Protein	15 g
Total fat	12 g
Monounsaturated fat	6.3 g
Polyunsaturated fat	3 g
Saturated fat	1.3 g
Fibre	9 g
Calcium	106 mg
Iron	4.4 mg
Magnesium	110 mg
Potassium	809 mg
Folic acid	225 mcg
Vitamin C	30 mg

Cantaloupe and strawberries with peppermint
Makes 4 servings

Half large ripe cantaloupe

500 ml (2 cups) fresh strawberries, washed and hulled

A few leaves of fresh peppermint

Use a melon baller to make balls from the cantaloupe.

In a bowl, mix the strawberries and cantaloupe balls, then garnish with small peppermint leaves.

If the peppermint leaves are too large, cut them with scissors.

Serve, preferably, at room temperature. Fresh fruits are always tastier when served this way.

NUTRITIONAL VALUE PER SERVING	
Calories	50
Protein	—
Total fat	—
Monounsaturated fat	—
Polyunsaturated fat	—
Saturated fat	—
Fibre	2 g
Calcium	19 mg
Iron	0.5 mg
Magnesium	16 mg
Potassium	352 mg
Folic acid	29 mcg
Vitamin C	78 mg

Menu 10
This colourful soup makes
a delicious first course.

People who like goat cheese will love this surprising lentil salad!

Winter squash soup

Lentil salad with goat cheese

Whole-wheat pita

Quick strawberry sorbet

Winter squash soup
Makes 4 servings

1 butternut squash, cut in half lengthwise

1 onion, chopped

15 ml (1 tbsp) extra-virgin olive oil

750 ml (3 cups) vegetable broth

1 sweet potato, cubed

Zest and juice of one orange

Salt and pepper

Plain yogurt

Chives, chopped

Preheat the oven to 190° C (375° F). On a cookie sheet, place the two halves of the squash flat and cook for 45 minutes or until the flesh is quite tender. Remove from the oven and let cool. Remove the flesh and set aside.

In a pot, sauté the onion in the olive oil for 3 minutes or until it is transparent. Add the vegetable broth, sweet potato, and squash. Bring to a boil, cover, and simmer for 25 minutes, or until the sweet potato is cooked.

Pour the mixture into the food processor or blender, and purée until smooth. Transfer back to the pot, then add the orange zest and juice. Season to taste and reheat.

Serve with 15 ml (1 tbsp) plain yogurt. Garnish with chives.

NUTRITIONAL VALUE PER SERVING	
Calories	149
Protein	4 g
Total fat	5 g
Monounsaturated fat	3 g
Polyunsaturated fat	—
Saturated fat	1 g
Fibre	4 g
Calcium	80 mg
Iron	1 mg
Magnesium	40 mg
Potassium	451 mg
Folic acid	34 mcg
Vitamin C	31 mg

Lentil salad with goat cheese
Makes 4 servings

500 ml (2 cups) cooked or canned lentils, drained
80 ml (1/3 cup) red onion, finely chopped
1 small cucumber, peeled and diced
250 ml (1 cup) cherry tomatoes, halved
170 g (6 oz) ripened goat cheese, crumbled
30 ml (2 tbsp) fresh dill, chopped coarsely
30 ml (2 tbsp) fresh parsley, chopped

Dressing
45 ml (3 tbsp) extra-virgin olive oil
30 ml (2 tbsp) white or red wine vinegar
15 ml (1 tbsp) Dijon mustard

In a large salad bowl, gently toss the lentils, onion, cucumber, tomatoes, goat cheese, dill, and parsley. Make the dressing by mixing the oil, vinegar, and mustard, then toss into the salad.

Marinate in the refrigerator or serve immediately. Serve on a nest of greens.

NUTRITIONAL VALUE PER SERVING	
Calories	402
Protein	20 g
Total fat	25 g
Monounsaturated fat	11 g
Polyunsaturated fat	2 g
Saturated fat	11 g
Fibre	6 g
Calcium	173 mg
Iron	5 mg
Magnesium	63 mg
Potassium	673 mg
Folic acid	209 mcg
Vitamin C	17 mg

Quick strawberry sorbet

Makes 4 servings

300 g (10 oz) frozen strawberries, not thawed

1 egg white

Juice of 1/2 lemon

80 ml (1/3 cup) sugar

Put all ingredients into the blender or food processor and purée.

Pour into a container, cover, and place in the freezer.

Serve chilled.

Variations: You can make this sorbet with other fruits. Blueberries, raspberries, and peaches are good choices.

NUTRITIONAL VALUE PER SERVING	
Calories	94
Protein	—
Total fat	—
Monounsaturated fat	—
Polyunsaturated fat	—
Saturated fat	—
Fibre	1 g
Calcium	13 mg
Iron	0.6 mg
Magnesium	10 mg
Potassium	133 mg
Folic acid	14 mcg
Vitamin C	35 mg

Menu II

This super-fast casserole
looks and tastes great.
The string-bean duo
is a sure-fire hit.

Super-fast tofu casserole with tomatoes and pesto

String bean duo cooked with ginger

Yogurt with strawberry coulis

Super-fast tofu casserole with tomatoes and pesto

Makes 3 servings

2 small or one large tomato

349 g (12.3 oz) extra-firm silken tofu or regular tofu*

6 thin slices Italian-flavour simulated cheese or regular cheese slices**

45 ml (3 tbsp) pesto

15 ml (1 tbsp) Parmesan, grated

Wash the tomatoes, then cut them into thin slices.

Then carefully cut the tofu into 12 slices.

Finally, cut the cheese slices in half.

In a Pyrex quiche dish, alternate tomato, tofu, and cheese slices around the edge of the dish. Spread a small amount of pesto on each slice of tofu. Keep alternating the slices, moving toward the centre of the dish, until there are no ingredients left.

Sprinkle with grated Parmesan. Cook at 200° C (400° F) for about 20 minutes.

* Silken tofu, even when extra-firm, is more difficult to slice than regular tofu, but it is softer. Both taste good!

** You can find sliced simulated cheese of different flavours with the soy products in refrigerator sections of supermarkets and natural-foods stores.

NUTRITIONAL VALUE PER SERVING	
Calories	310
Protein	26 g
Total fat	20 g
Monounsaturated fat	7 g
Polyunsaturated fat	3.8 g
Saturated fat	5.3 g
Fibre	2 g
Calcium	564 mg
Iron	7.7 mg
Magnesium	139 mg
Potassium	395 mg
Folic acid	36 mcg
Vitamin C	17 mg

String bean duo cooked with ginger
Makes 4 servings

500 g (1 lb) green and yellow string beans*
15 ml (1 tbsp) nut or sesame oil
15 ml (1 tbsp) fresh ginger, chopped
125 ml (1/2 cup) cashew nuts, finely chopped
Salt and ground pepper

Steam the string beans briefly until al dente.

In a small pot, heat the oil over low heat. Add the ginger and nuts and cook, stirring, for one minute. Incorporate the string beans and reheat.

Season to taste and serve.

*This recipe can be made using fresh asparagus sliced on the diagonal. That would be an asparagus solo!

NUTRITIONAL VALUE PER SERVING	
Calories	174
Protein	5 g
Total fat	12 g
Monounsaturated fat	5.7 g
Polyunsaturated fat	3.7 g
Saturated fat	2 g
Fibre	5 g
Calcium	55 mg
Iron	2.4 mg
Magnesium	79 mg
Potassium	370 mg
Folic acid	58 mcg
Vitamin C	20 mg

Menu 12

**This meatless lasagna filled
with protein and iron will
become a family favourite.**

Served with coleslaw and a kiwi dessert,
it is a winning combination!

Vegetarian lasagna*

Fresh coleslaw

Kiwi slices with vanilla or honey-sweetened yogurt

* When you use precooked whole-wheat pasta sold in the supermarket, this dish is
much faster to make. Making lasagna practically becomes child's play!

Vegetarian lasagna
Makes 8 servings

12 sheets of whole-wheat lasagna pasta (precooked, if you can find it)

15 ml (1 tbsp) extra-virgin olive oil

1 onion, chopped

1 or 2 cloves garlic, chopped

625 ml (2 1/2 cups) homemade or store-bought tomato sauce

1 bay leaf

5 ml (1 tsp) dried oregano

30 ml (2 tbsp) fresh parsley, chopped

1 egg, beaten

250 ml (1 cup) ricotta or cottage cheese

284 g (10 oz) fresh spinach, cooked, drained, and chopped

340 g (12 oz) regular tofu, crumbled in a blender or food processor

125 ml (1/2 cup) Parmesan, grated

Salt and pepper to taste

340 g (3/4 lb) part-skim mozzarella cheese, thinly sliced

Cook the pasta according to the instructions on the package or use precooked pasta.

In a pot, heat the oil over medium heat and brown the onion and garlic. Pour the tomato sauce into this mixture, then add the bay leaf and oregano. Simmer a few minutes over low heat so the flavours blend well. Remove from heat and add half the chopped parsley. Set aside.

In a large bowl, mix the egg, ricotta or cottage cheese, cooked spinach, crumbled tofu, half the Parmesan, and the rest of the chopped parsley. Season to taste. Set aside.

In a lightly greased 23 x 33 cm (9 x 13 cm) oven-safe dish, spread one third of the tomato sauce, then place 3 lasagna pasta sheets. Top with half of the spinach-tofu mixture, press down well, and cover with slices of mozzarella. Place three more pasta sheets, another third of the tomato sauce, and mozzarella slices. Then place another layer of pasta, cover with the other half of the spinach-tofu mixture, and finish with slices of mozzarella. Cover with the rest of the pasta, tomato sauce, mozzarella, and the rest of the Parmesan.

Cook in a preheated oven at 180° C (350° F) for 30 to 40 minutes or until the sauce bubbles and the top is golden. Garnish with parsley and serve.

NUTRITIONAL VALUE PER SERVING	
Calories	350
Protein	28 g
Total fat	18 g
Monounsaturated fat	6 g
Polyunsaturated fat	2 g
Saturated fat	9 g
Fibre	4 g
Calcium	633 mg
Iron	5 mg
Magnesium	125 mg
Potassium	711 mg
Folic acid	105 mcg
Vitamin C	24 mg

Menu 13
A knock-out to discover!

This Indian delight is an adventurous,
festive blend of legumes, vegetables, dried fruit, and lovely spices.

Indian delight

Basmati brown rice

Endive salad

Orange and strawberry jelly

Indian delight

Makes 5 servings

625 ml (2 1/2 cups) cooked legumes (chickpeas or white beans)

30 ml (2 tbsp) olive oil

2 onions, thinly sliced

4 carrots, peeled and sliced on the diagonal

225 g (1/2 lb) fresh asparagus, sliced on the diagonal

15 ml (1 tbsp) curry powder

45 ml (3 tbsp) flour*

300 ml (1 1/4 cups) chicken broth

180 ml (3/4 cup) golden raisins

180 ml (3/4 cup) unsalted, roasted cashew nuts

30 ml (2 tbsp) apricot jam

15 ml (1 tbsp) homemade fruit tamale ketchup**
or fruit relish

Sauté the onion, carrots, and asparagus in the oil until the onion is transparent. Add the curry powder and flour. Cook one minute. Incorporate the legumes and broth; cook until the carrots are tender but not soft.

Add the raisins, nuts, jam, and ketchup, and cook until the raisins are tender. Add broth, if necessary, but retain the thick consistency of a stew.

Serve with brown rice.

NUTRITIONAL VALUE PER SERVING	
Calories	491
Protein	16 g
Total fat	18 g
Monounsaturated fat	10.8 g
Polyunsaturated fat	3.1 g
Saturated fat	3 g
Fibre	10 g
Calcium	121 mg
Iron	6 mg
Magnesium	147 mg
Potassium	1,101 mg
Folic acid	208 mcg
Vitamin C	16 mg

* You can replace the flour with 30 ml (2 tbsp) cornstarch or arrowroot.
** Fruit tamale ketchup can be made in September when tomatoes, peaches, and pears are abundant.

Orange and strawberry jelly
Makes 4 servings

1 packet unflavoured gelatin

60 ml (1/4 cup) cold water

250 ml (1 cup) fresh ripe or thawed frozen strawberries

180 ml (3/4 cup) frozen orange juice concentrate, no sugar added, undiluted

180 ml (3/4 cup) water

125 ml (1/2 cup) boiling water

In a large bowl, let the gelatin swell in the cold water for 5 minutes. In the blender or food processor, place the strawberries, the orange juice, and the 180 ml (3/4 cup) of water. Purée until smooth.

Pour 125 ml (1/2 cup) boiling water on the softened gelatin, then stir to dissolve. Pour the strawberry-orange purée into the gelatin mixture and stir. Let set in the refrigerator for several hours.

NUTRITIONAL VALUE PER SERVING	
Calories	97
Protein	—
Total fat	—
Monounsaturated fat	—
Polyunsaturated fat	—
Saturated fat	—
Fibre	1 g
Calcium	23 mg
Iron	0.3 mg
Magnesium	22 mg
Potassium	427 mg
Folic acid	90 mcg
Vitamin C	96 mg

Menu 14
During the holiday season, surprise your friends with this meatless tourtière.

Don't tell anyone what ingredients you used for
this traditional French-Canadian dish.
Try this pie crust recipe and do away with hydrogenated fat.

Tofu tourtière with whole-wheat pie crust

Minute ratatouille

Baked apple

Tofu tourtière with whole-wheat pie crust

Makes 5 servings

Filling

454 g (1 lb) regular tofu

1 onion, finely chopped

4 garlic cloves, crushed

30 ml (2 tbsp) olive oil

2 ml (1/2 tsp) ground cloves

5 ml (1 tsp) dried thyme

5 ml (1 tsp) dried savory

60 ml (4 tbsp) light soy sauce

60 ml (4 tbsp) water

45 ml (3 tbsp) torula yeast*

Salt and ground pepper, to taste

Crumble the tofu in the food processor or by passing it through a food grinder. In a large pot, sauté the onion and garlic in olive oil for a few minutes to soften. Add the other ingredients and cook for about 10 minutes. Correct the seasoning to taste.

Pour the mixture into a whole-wheat pie shell. Cover with pastry.

Bake at 220° C (425° F) for 10 minutes, then reduce the temperature to 190° C (375° F) and bake another 30 minutes.

* You can find torula yeast in natural-foods stores.

Whole-wheat pie pastry

(with no hydrogenated fat)

Makes two 23 cm (9 in) pie shells

625 ml (2 1/2 cups) whole-wheat pastry flour

5 ml (1 tsp) sugar

5 ml (1 tsp) salt

30 ml (2 tbsp) butter

125 ml (1/2 cup) canola oil

60 to 90 ml (4 to 6 tbsp) ice water

Mix the flour, sugar, and salt in a bowl.

Over low heat, melt the butter for about 30 seconds. Pour into a small bowl and let cool, then incorporate the oil. With a fork, work the oil and butter into the flour mixture until it has a granular texture.

Add just enough ice water for the pastry to form a ball. Divide the pastry into two balls. Flatten each ball and place between two sheets of waxed paper. Roll the pastry until it has the desired shape. Take the paper off the top and reverse the pastry into the pie plate. Mould well to pie plate.

Refrigerate before cooking, if desired.

NUTRITIONAL VALUE FOR ONE SERVING OF TOURTIÈRE	
Calories	637
Protein	20g
Total fat	39 g
Monounsaturated fat	21 g
Polyunsaturated fat	10 g
Saturated fat	6 g
Fibre	11g
Calcium	154 mg
Iron	9.4 mg
Magnesium	205 mg
Potassium	579 mg
Folic acid	304 mcg
Vitamin C	3 mg

Note: This recipe came to us years ago from a patient whose name we can't remember, but we are still thanking her! We were thrilled to rediscover it.

Minute ratatouille
Makes 4 servings

250 ml (1 cup) red or green bell peppers, cut into thin strips

250 ml (1 cup) eggplant, cubed

250 ml (1 cup) zucchini, sliced in rounds

250 ml (1 cup) Italian tomatoes, fresh or canned, cut into pieces

30 ml (2 tbsp) olive oil

2 to 3 garlic cloves, crushed

5 ml (1 tsp) dried thyme

Salt and pepper to taste

In a large, microwave-safe bowl, mix all ingredients well.

Cover and cook 8 minutes on high, turning the bowl midway through cooking. Or bake in a conventional oven for about 1 hour at 180° C (350° F).

NUTRITIONAL VALUE PER SERVING	
Calories	99
Protein	1.6 g
Total fat	7 g
Monounsaturated fat	5 g
Polyunsaturated fat	0.7 g
Saturated fat	1 g
Fibre	2.6 g
Calcium	41 mg
Iron	1.3 mg
Magnesium	22 mg
Potassium	349 mg
Folic acid	21 mcg
Vitamin C	63 mg

Menu 15

This unusual and fragrant stew
will quickly become a
household favourite.

Chickpea and vegetable stew

Grilled whole-wheat pita

Sliced cucumbers with tzatziki (made with yogurt)

Prunes with a touch of orange

Chickpea and vegetable stew
Makes 4 servings

500 ml (2 cups) vegetable broth

1 onion, chopped

3 cloves garlic, chopped

375 ml (1 1/2 cups) zucchini, diced

1 large sweet potato, peeled and diced

250 ml (1 cup) red bell pepper, diced

250 ml (1 cup) green bell pepper, diced

250 ml (1 cup) diced canned tomatoes, with juice

5 ml (1 tsp) cinnamon

5 ml (1 tsp) ground coriander

2 ml (1/2 tsp) cumin

A pinch of cayenne

Salt and pepper to taste

15 ml (1 tbsp) lemon juice

540 ml (19 oz) canned chickpeas, drained

30 ml (2 tbsp) fresh parsley, finely chopped

Pour 300 ml (1 1/4 cups) of broth into a large pot, then add the onion and garlic. Cook over medium-high heat for 5 minutes, until the onion is transparent.

Add the zucchini, sweet potato, peppers, tomatoes, cinnamon, coriander, cumin, cayenne, salt, and pepper. Bring the mixture to a boil and let simmer over medium-high heat for 5 minutes.

NUTRITIONAL VALUE PER SERVING	
Calories	411
Protein	17 g
Total fat	3.7 g
Monounsaturated fat	0.6 g
Polyunsaturated fat	1.4 g
Saturated fat	0.4 g
Fibre	11 g
Calcium	120 mg
Iron	5 mg
Magnesium	89 mg
Potassium	862 mg
Folic acid	216 mcg
Vitamin C	96 mg

Add the rest of the broth and the lemon juice, bring to a boil, cover, and simmer over low heat until the vegetables are tender, about 5 minutes. Add the chickpeas and cook just enough to heat them.

Sprinkle with the fresh parsley.

Prunes with a touch of orange
Makes 4 servings

24 prunes
300 ml (1 1/4 cups) orange juice

Over low heat, poach the prunes in the orange juice for about 30 minutes to soften and flavour them. Serve lukewarm or cold.

NUTRITIONAL VALUE PER SERVING	
Calories	156
Protein	2 g
Total fat	—
Monounsaturated fat	—
Polyunsaturated fat	—
Saturated fat	—
Fibre	5 g
Calcium	34 mg
Iron	1.4 mg
Magnesium	31 mg
Potassium	533 mg
Folic acid	26 mcg
Vitamin C	41 mg

Menu 16

This oven-baked spaghetti can be prepared in advance and baked when you get home from work.

As a variation, try a different legume.

Oven-baked spaghetti and lentils

Waldorf salad

Melon melody

Oven-baked spaghetti and lentils
Makes 6 servings

250 ml (1 cup) dried lentils (du Puy, brown, or green)
750 ml (3 cups) chicken broth or water
225 g (1/2 lb) fresh mushrooms
10 ml (2 tsp) olive oil
15 ml (1 tbsp) fresh oregano, finely chopped
or 5 ml (1 tsp) dried oregano
170 g (6 oz) whole-wheat spaghetti
500 ml (2 cups) well-seasoned tomato sauce
60 ml (1/4 cup) whole-wheat bread crumbs
60 ml (1/4 cup) walnuts, ground

Rinse and sort the lentils and cook them in the broth or water for about 30 minutes or until the lentils are tender. Drain.

Wash and dry the mushrooms and cut into pieces. Sauté them in the olive oil, season with fresh chopped oregano, then mix with the cooked lentils.

Cook the pasta in boiling water, then drain it.

Drip or spray a bit of olive oil on an oven-proof dish, then place half the pasta in the dish. Cover with half of the cooked lentils and mushrooms. Cover with half of the sauce. Repeat these steps, finishing with the sauce. Sprinkle with bread crumbs and walnuts.

Bake at 180° C (350° F) for 45 to 50 minutes.

NUTRITIONAL VALUE PER SERVING	
Calories	311
Protein	18 g
Total fat	7 g
Monounsaturated fat	1.9 g
Polyunsaturated fat	2.3 g
Saturated fat	0.7 g
Fibre	10 g
Calcium	55 mg
Iron	5.4 mg
Magnesium	90 mg
Potassium	846 mg
Folic acid	171 mcg
Vitamin C	15 mg

Waldorf salad

Makes 4 servings

3 to 4 medium McIntosh apples, unpeeled, cubed

Juice of 1/2 lemon

250 ml (1 cup) celery, cut in pieces of just over 1 cm (1/2 in)

60 ml (1/4 cup) walnuts, chopped coarsely

30 ml (2 tbsp) fresh herbs, chopped: chives, parsley, or coriander

Sprinkle the apple cubes with lemon juice and mix well. Add the other ingredients and toss.

Serve with 15 ml (1 tbsp) tofu mayonnaise (see recipe on p. 48).

NUTRITIONAL VALUE PER SERVING	
Calories	145
Protein	3.3 g
Total fat	6.4 g
Monounsaturated fat	2.2 g
Polyunsaturated fat	3 g
Saturated fat	0.6 g
Fibre	3.2 g
Calcium	44 mg
Iron	1.4 mg
Magnesium	39 mg
Potassium	308 mg
Folic acid	18 mcg
Vitamin C	14 mg

Melon melody
Makes 6 servings

500 ml (2 cups) balls of melons in season, including cantaloupe
250 ml (1 cup) orange juice
60 ml (1/4 cup) lime juice
30 ml (2 tbsp) honey
15 ml (1 tbsp) fresh mint, chopped

Put the melon balls in a serving bowl, then sprinkle with orange juice, lime juice, and honey.

Garnish with fresh chopped mint, then let sit for the flavours to blend.

NUTRITIONAL VALUE PER SERVING	
Calories	103
Protein	—
Total fat	—
Monounsaturated fat	—
Polyunsaturated fat	—
Saturated fat	—
Fibre	1 g
Calcium	21 mg
Iron	0.4 mg
Magnesium	22 mg
Potassium	503 mg
Folic acid	43 mcg
Vitamin C	69 mg

Menu I7
A quick Greek-style meal
built around a soup

An excellent source of iron and protein. The fruit served
with strawberry coulis adds freshness and a healthy dose of vitamin C.

Tofu and fennel soup with sun-dried tomato pesto
Romaine lettuce and Greek olive salad, garlic vinaigrette
Whole-wheat bun
Trio of summer berries or quarter cantaloupe with strawberry coulis

Tofu and fennel soup with sun-dried tomato pesto
Makes 4 servings

15 ml (1 tbsp) extra-virgin olive oil

1 onion, chopped

1 bulb of fennel,* thinly sliced

1 litre (4 cups) vegetable broth

3 fresh tomatoes, diced

349 g (12.3 oz) firm silken tofu, cubed

Salt and pepper to taste

20 ml (4 tsp) sun-dried tomato pesto (can be found commercially)

In a pot, heat the oil over low heat and sauté the onion and fennel for 5 minutes. Add the vegetable broth, fresh tomatoes, and tofu. Bring the mixture to a boil, cover, and simmer for 30 minutes. Season to taste.

Serve the soup hot and garnish each portion with 5 ml (1 tsp) of pesto.

* Fennel adds a taste of licorice. If you can't find it, replace it with 4 celery stalks, cut in pieces.

NUTRITIONAL VALUE PER SERVING	
Calories	198
Protein	15 g
Total fat	12 g
Monounsaturated fat	5.2 g
Polyunsaturated fat	3.3 g
Saturated fat	1.8 g
Fibre	4 g
Calcium	177 mg
Iron	6 mg
Magnesium	127 mg
Potassium	613 mg
Folic acid	49 mcg
Vitamin C	26 mg

Menu 18
This lentil stew is tasty and stylish.
You will want to make it
more than once!

Lentil stew with apples and almonds

Fresh asparagus with vinaigrette

Rhubarb and strawberry compote with ginger and vanilla

Lentil stew with apples and almonds

Makes 4 servings

15 ml (1 tbsp) extra-virgin olive oil

1 clove garlic, chopped

1 onion, chopped

4 carrots, diced

1 stalk celery, diced

10 ml (2 tsp) curry powder

10 ml (2 tsp) light tamari sauce

250 ml (1 cup) butternut squash, peeled and cubed

250 ml (1 cup) green string beans, cut in pieces

125 ml (1/2 cup) apple, diced

45 ml (3 tbsp) almonds, chopped

30 ml (2 tbsp) raisins

500 ml (2 cups) vegetable broth

500 ml (2 cups) small brown lentils, cooked

1 zucchini, sliced

30 ml (2 tbsp) fresh parsley, chopped

NUTRITIONAL VALUE PER SERVING	
Calories	323
Protein	15 g
Total fat	8.5 g
Monounsaturated fat	5 g
Polyunsaturated fat	1.4 g
Saturated fat	1 g
Fibre	12 g
Calcium	120 mg
Iron	5.7 mg
Magnesium	111 mg
Potassium	1,153 mg
Folic acid	245 mcg
Vitamin C	32 mg

In a large pot, heat the oil over low heat and sauté the garlic, onion, carrots, and celery for 5 minutes. Add the curry powder and tamari sauce, and incorporate the squash, string beans, apple, 30 ml (2 tbsp) almonds, and raisins. Pour in the vegetable broth and add the lentils. Bring to a boil. Lower the heat and simmer for 20 minutes, stirring often.

Add the zucchini and continue cooking 5 to 10 minutes or until tender. Garnish with the rest of the almonds and the fresh parsley, then serve.

Rhubarb and strawberry compote with ginger and vanilla

500 g (1 lb) fresh rhubarb, cut in pieces

300 ml (1 1/4 cups) water

Zests of 1/2 lemon and 1/2 orange, in strips

70 g (2 1/2 oz) fresh ginger, peeled and cut into thin rounds

125 ml (1/2 cup) sugar

1 vanilla bean, split lengthwise

10 whole fresh strawberries

In a large pot, make a syrup with the water, zests, ginger, sugar, and vanilla.

Bring the syrup to a boil and boil several minutes, then add the rhubarb and cook over low heat, uncovered, about 20 minutes. Add the fresh strawberries for the last 5 minutes of cooking. This dish is good lukewarm or cold.

Note: This compote is excellent with plain yogurt.

NUTRITIONAL VALUE PER SERVING	
Calories	150
Protein	—
Total fat	—
Monounsaturated fat	—
Polyunsaturated fat	—
Saturated fat	—
Fibre	2.6 g
Calcium	62 mg
Iron	0.5 mg
Magnesium	22 mg
Potassium	364 mg
Folic acid	20 mcg
Vitamin C	51 mg

Menu 19

Tofu gives a velvety texture –
and lots of key nutrients –
to this cream of mushroom soup.

Silken cream of mushroom soup

Fougasse* with black olives

Spinach salad with cherry tomatoes

Broiled pink grapefruit** with a touch of maple

* Fougasse is an olive "ladder" bread that originates from Provence in France
and can be found at bakeries or in the bakery section of supermarkets.
** Broiled pink grapefruit with maple is prepared very easily: halve a grapefruit
and separate the membranes with a small knife. Sprinkle with 5 ml (1 tsp) of
maple sugar or maple syrup, then broil for a few minutes.

Silken cream of mushroom soup

Makes 2 servings

15 ml (1 tbsp) extra-virgin olive oil

1 onion, chopped

1 clove garlic, chopped

225 g (1/2 lb) café (brown) mushrooms, cleaned and sliced

5 ml (1 tsp) dried thyme

125 ml (1/2 cup) white wine

349 g (12.3 oz) soft silken tofu

250 ml (1 cup) vegetable broth

5 ml (1 tsp) light tamari sauce

A pinch of cayenne

Salt and pepper to taste

In a pot, heat the oil over low heat and sauté the onion and garlic for 3 minutes or until the onion is transparent. Add the mushrooms and thyme. Cook for 5 minutes, pour in the white wine, and simmer for 5 more minutes.

During this time, place the tofu in the bowl of the food processor or blender and liquefy. Incorporate the vegetable broth, then mix together.

Add a ladleful of the cooking liquid from the mushrooms to the tofu mixture and mix again. Incorporate this mixture with the mushrooms, then add the tamari sauce and cayenne. Season with salt and pepper to taste. Reheat the soup without boiling and serve.

NUTRITIONAL VALUE PER SERVING	
Calories	273
Protein	17 g
Total fat	12.6 g
Monounsaturated fat	6 g
Polyunsaturated fat	3.8 g
Saturated fat	1 g
Fibre	2.6 g
Calcium	37 mg
Iron	2.7 mg
Magnesium	26 mg
Potassium	901 mg
Folic acid	34 mcg
Vitamin C	8 mg

Menu 20
This spicy bean salad travels
well in a lunchbox or to a picnic.

Spicy red kidney bean salad

Grated celery root salad with mint

Whole wheat or flaxseed rolls

Oranges Ambrosia

Spicy red kidney bean salad

Makes 6 servings

1 litre (4 cups) red kidney beans, cooked or canned

6 green onions, finely chopped

1 clove garlic, chopped

30 ml (2 tbsp) tomato paste

30 ml (2 tbsp) wine vinegar

60 ml (1/4 cup) olive oil

10 ml (2 tsp) Dijon mustard

Salt and pepper to taste

Put the red kidney beans, green onions, and garlic in a salad bowl and mix lightly.

Mix all the other ingredients in a small bowl and pour onto the beans. If desired, let marinate a few hours in the refrigerator. Serve on a nest of greens.

NUTRITIONAL VALUE PER SERVING	
Calories	375
Protein	17 g
Total fat	15 g
Monounsaturated fat	10 g
Polyunsaturated fat	1.8 g
Saturated fat	2 g
Fibre	15 g
Calcium	69 mg
Iron	6 mg
Magnesium	90 mg
Potassium	879 mg
Folic acid	250 mcg
Vitamin C	8 mg

Grated celery root salad with mint
Makes 6 servings

1 small celery root (celeriac), grated in the food processor or grinder
375 ml (1 1/2 cups) fresh peppermint, chopped
60 ml (1/4 cup) fresh Italian parsley, chopped

Vinaigrette
60 ml (1/4 cup) cold-pressed walnut or hazelnut oil
30 ml (2 tbsp) plain yogurt
15 ml (1 tbsp) cider vinegar
2 ml (1/2 tsp) sea salt

In a bowl, mix all the ingredients for the celery root (celeriac) salad.

Using a small whisk, mix all the ingredients for the vinaigrette. Add the dressing to the celery root, then toss well.

NUTRITIONAL VALUE PER SERVING	
Calories	161
Protein	1.7 g
Total fat	9.6 g
Monounsaturated fat	2.2 g
Polyunsaturated fat	5.8 g
Saturated fat	0.9 g
Fibre	4 g
Calcium	60 mg
Iron	1.5 mg
Magnesium	22 mg
Potassium	288 mg
Folic acid	32 mcg
Vitamin C	29 mg

Oranges Ambrosia

Makes 4 servings

4 navel oranges

125 ml (1/2 cup) orange juice

60 ml (1/4 cup) grated coconut

Peel the oranges down to the flesh, then cut into thin slices. Pour the orange juice onto them and sprinkle with grated coconut — roasted, if desired.

NUTRITIONAL VALUE PER SERVING	
Calories	194
Protein	1 g
Total fat	6 g
Monounsaturated fat	—
Polyunsaturated fat	—
Saturated fat	5 g
Fibre	4 g
Calcium	64 mg
Iron	1.1 mg
Magnesium	35 mg
Potassium	460 mg
Folic acid	69 mcg
Vitamin C	90 mg

Menu 21

The orange sauce in the tofu
sauté is divine.

This recipe is simple to make and loaded with iron. Try it out!

Orange-scented tofu sauté on a bed of watercress
Brown rice and barley pilaf
Steamed broccoli
Plain yogurt with strawberry coulis

Orange-scented tofu sauté on a bed of watercress

Makes 3 servings

30 ml (2 tbsp) extra-virgin olive oil

349 g (12.3 oz) extra-firm silken tofu, well drained and sliced

1 bunch watercress, washed, the thickest stems removed

15 ml (1 tbsp) whole sesame seeds

10 ml (2 tsp) fresh ginger, peeled and chopped

1 clove garlic, chopped

60 ml (1/4 cup) freshly squeezed orange juice

10 ml (2 tsp) light tamari sauce

2 ml (1/2 tsp) roasted-sesame oil

In a large nonstick pan, heat 15 ml (1 tbsp) olive oil over medium heat and sauté the tofu slices for 3 minutes on each side or until they are golden. Remove from pan and keep warm.

Heat the rest of the olive oil and sauté the watercress for a few minutes, or until it begins to wilt. Transfer the greens onto a serving dish, sprinkle with sesame seeds, and place the tofu slices on them.

In the still-hot pan, simmer the rest of the ingredients for 1 minute, then pour the sauce over the tofu.

NUTRITIONAL VALUE PER SERVING	
Calories	286
Protein	15 g
Total fat	17 g
Monounsaturated fat	8.8 g
Polyunsaturated fat	4.9 g
Saturated fat	2.4 g
Fibre	2 g
Calcium	186 mg
Iron	7 mg
Magnesium	139 mg
Potassium	286 mg
Folic acid	29 mcg
Vitamin C	20 mg

Brown rice and barley pilaf
Makes 4 servings

500 ml (2 cups) chicken broth

125 ml (1/2 cup) pot barley*

125 ml (1/2 cup) brown rice

30 ml (2 tbsp) celery, finely chopped

30 ml (2 tbsp) green or red bell pepper, finely chopped

30 ml (2 tbsp) onion, finely chopped

60 ml (1/4 cup) parsley, finely chopped

60 ml (1/4 cup) pine nuts, roasted

60 ml (1/4 cup) whole sesame seeds

Put the barley, rice, and chicken broth into a pot and bring to a boil.

Reduce heat and add the chopped vegetables. Cover and cook over low heat for 45 minutes.

Add the parsley, pine nuts, and sesame seeds.

Mix and serve.

NUTRITIONAL VALUE PER SERVING	
Calories	190
Protein	8 g
Total fat	8.9 g
Monounsaturated fat	3.3 g
Polyunsaturated fat	3.7 g
Saturated fat	1.4 g
Fibre	6 g
Calcium	95 mg
Iron	2.7 mg
Magnesium	77 mg
Potassium	338 mg
Folic acid	26 mcg
Vitamin C	8 mg

* Pot barley is a very good source of soluble fibre, which can lower your cholesterol level. It takes about 1 hour to cook and it can be soaked before cooking. For more flavour, cook it in chicken broth.

Menu 22
A light and festive buffet-style
meal, to be served cold

At Hallowe'en, make the salad with black beans
and orange bell peppers — it's spooky!

Black bean salad with multicolour bell peppers
in a cumin and coriander vinaigrette
Wild rice salad with roasted hazelnuts
Yogurt flan with raspberry coulis

Black bean salad with multicolour peppers
Makes 4 servings

750 ml (3 cups) canned black beans, drained
125 ml (1/2 cup) red bell pepper, diced fine
125 ml (1/2 cup) yellow bell pepper, diced fine
125 ml (1/2 cup) green bell pepper, diced fine
125 ml (1/2 cup) celery, diced fine
A few sprigs of fresh coriander for garnish

Cumin and coriander vinaigrette
15 ml (1 tbsp) lemon juice
5 ml (1 tsp) lemon zest
15 ml (1 tbsp) white wine vinegar
2 ml (1/2 tsp) salt
1 clove garlic, finely chopped
2 ml (1/2 tsp) ground cumin seeds
2 ml (1/2 tsp) ground coriander seeds
1 ml (1/4 tsp) paprika
75 ml (5 tbsp) extra-virgin olive oil
15 ml (1 tbsp) fresh mint, chopped
15 ml (1 tbsp) fresh coriander, chopped

NUTRITIONAL VALUE PER SERVING	
Calories	361
Protein	15 g
Total fat	18 g
Monounsaturated fat	12.7 g
Polyunsaturated fat	1.8 g
Saturated fat	2.5 g
Fibre	14 g
Calcium	113 mg
Iron	10.6 mg
Magnesium	103 mg
Potassium	619 mg
Folic acid	217 mcg
Vitamin C	65 mg

In a salad bowl, mix all salad ingredients well.

Mix all ingredients for the dressing and stir. Pour onto the salad and toss thoroughly.

Yogurt flan with raspberry coulis
Makes 6 servings

1 packet unflavoured gelatin

60 ml (1/4 cup) cold water

375 ml (1 1/2 cups) skim or 1% milk

125 ml (1/2 cup) sugar

550 ml (2 1/4 cups) plain yogurt

5 ml (1 tsp) vanilla

Let the gelatin swell in the water for 10 minutes. In a pot, heat the milk and the sugar together, then stir to dissolve the sugar.

Remove from heat and add the softened gelatin, stirring to dissolve it.

Once the gelatin is dissolved, pour this mixture into a large bowl and let cool 5 minutes. Add the yogurt, stirring gently, and flavour with vanilla.

Pour into a 1.25 litre (5 cup) mould that has been run under cold water. Refrigerate at least 2 1/2 hours. Unmould the flan and serve with raspberry coulis or fresh fruit.

NUTRITIONAL VALUE PER SERVING	
Calories	255
Protein	8 g
Total fat	1.6 g
Monounsaturated fat	0.4 g
Polyunsaturated fat	0.2 g
Saturated fat	1 g
Fibre	4 g
Calcium	268 mg
Iron	0.8 mg
Magnesium	37 mg
Potassium	445 mg
Folic acid	40 mcg
Vitamin C	18 mg

Raspberry coulis
Makes 250 ml (1 cup)

2 300 g (10 oz) boxes of frozen raspberries, thawed and drained
15 ml (1 tbsp) fine sugar
15 ml (1 tbsp) lemon juice

Purée the fruit and pass through a strainer to eliminate seeds.

Add the sugar and lemon juice, then mix. Serve with the flan or spoon over the flan.

Note: The yogurt flan literally melts in your mouth. Serve it in an elegant mould or dessert bowls. It is just as delicious with fresh fruits as with a fruit coulis.

Menu 23

The main dish, prepared with soy-
based cheese and peanut sauce, is a
delectable discovery.

Roll the filling in a leaf of romaine lettuce or a
whole-wheat Azim bread and you have a wrap!

Bell pepper rings
Spring wrap with soy-based cheese and peanut sauce
Orange and yogurt smoothie

Spring wrap with soy-based cheese and peanut sauce

Makes 2 servings

Peanut sauce*

60 ml (1/4 cup) natural crunchy peanut butter

60 ml (1/4 cup) honey

45 ml (3 tbsp) pale miso

30 ml (2 tbsp) water

30 ml (2 tbsp) fresh lime juice

2 whole-wheat pitas or Azim breads

or 2 large leaves of romaine lettuce

6 slices Italian-flavour soy-based cheese,** cut in strips

1/4 cucumber, seeded and sliced very thin lengthwise

1 carrot, grated

30 ml (2 tbsp) fresh mint, chopped

30 ml (2 tbsp) fresh coriander, chopped, or Italian parsley

In a bowl, mix the peanut butter, honey, miso, water, and lime juice.

Spread the sauce on the inside of the pitas or Azim breads, then fill with the strips of simulated cheese, cucumber slices, grated carrot, mint, and coriander.

*   To make things go faster, Thai Kitchen makes a very tasty peanut sauce. You can find it in fine grocery stores and natural-foods stores, but it's a bit pricey!

** You can find sliced soy-based cheeses in different flavours with the soy products in refrigerated sections of supermarkets or natural-foods stores.

NUTRITIONAL VALUE PER SERVING	
Calories	574
Protein	28 g
Total fat	23 g
Monounsaturated fat	7 g
Polyunsaturated fat	5.3 g
Saturated fat	3 g
Fibre	9 g
Calcium	372 mg
Iron	13 mg
Magnesium	99 mg
Potassium	483 mg
Folic acid	54 mcg
Vitamin C	10 mg

Orange and yogurt smoothie
Makes 2 servings

300 ml (1 1/4 cups) plain yogurt

90 ml (6 tbsp) frozen concentrated orange juice

In the blender or food processor, whip the yogurt and orange juice. Serve in two glasses.

Note: The homemade version isn't as sweet as the commercial version.

NUTRITIONAL VALUE PER SERVING	
Calories	176
Protein	11 g
Total fat	2.5 g
Monounsaturated fat	0.6 g
Polyunsaturated fat	0.6 g
Saturated fat	1 g
Fibre	—
Calcium	374 mg
Iron	1 mg
Magnesium	55 mg
Potassium	814 mg
Folic acid	120 mcg
Vitamin C	85 mg

Menu 24
A sunny weekend breakfast

Don't forget that eggs belong in a healthy
diet for a part-time vegetarian.

Orange quarters

Cockadoodle croquettes!

Apple and oatmeal muffins

Café au lait

Cockadoodle croquettes!
Makes 4 servings

250 ml (1 cup) mixed grated vegetables, your choice (onion, sweet potato, and zucchini, for example)

6 eggs, beaten

125 ml (1/2 cup) milk or unflavoured soy beverage

30 g (1 oz) Gruyère cheese, grated

Salt and pepper to taste

Lightly grease 6 125 ml (1/2 cup) compartments in a muffin tin.

Drain the grated vegetables thoroughly to remove as much moisture as possible and pour into the muffin tin.

In a large bowl, mix the beaten eggs, milk or soy beverage, and cheese, and season to taste. Pour onto the vegetables in the muffin tin.

Bake in an oven preheated to 200° C (400° F) for 15 minutes or until the croquettes are cooked.

NUTRITIONAL VALUE PER SERVING	
Calories	204
Protein	16 g
Total fat	12 g
Monounsaturated fat	4.5 g
Polyunsaturated fat	1.5 g
Saturated fat	4.7 g
Fibre	1 g
Calcium	163 mg
Iron	1.5 mg
Magnesium	22 mg
Potassium	248 mg
Folic acid	55 mcg
Vitamin C	4 mg

Apple and oatmeal muffins

Makes 12 muffins

180 ml (3/4 cup) boiling water

125 ml (1/2 cup) rolled oats

125 ml (1/2 cup) oat bran

250 ml (1 cup) whole-wheat flour

15 ml (1 tbsp) baking powder

2 ml (1/2 tsp) salt

60 ml (1/4 cup) skim-milk powder

60 ml (1/4 cup) wheat germ

2 eggs

30 ml (2 tbsp) cold-pressed canola oil

60 ml (1/4 cup) cold water

60 ml (1/4 cup) molasses

250 ml (1 cup) unpeeled apples, washed and cut into small pieces

60 ml (1/4 cup) whole sesame seeds

Pour the boiling water on the rolled oats and oat bran and let cool.

Grease the muffin tins and preheat the oven to 200° C (400° F).

In a large bowl, mix the flour with all the other dry ingredients except the sesame seeds.

Beat together the eggs, oil, cold water, and molasses. Add the warm oats, then the apple pieces. Incorporate the dry ingredients and mix just enough to moisten all the ingredients.

Pour into the muffin tin. Sprinkle with sesame seeds.

Bake 20 to 25 minutes. Serve warm.

NUTRITIONAL VALUE PER SERVING	
Calories	138
Protein	5 g
Total fat	5.4 g
Monounsaturated fat	2.4 g
Polyunsaturated fat	1.7 g
Saturated fat	0.7 g
Fibre	3 g
Calcium	64 mg
Iron	1.7 mg
Magnesium	61 mg
Potassium	264 mg
Folic acid	21 mcg
Vitamin C	—

Menu 25
A Mediterranean-style meal, simple and easy to pack for lunch!

Mediterranean-style lentil salad

Whole-wheat Azim bread* or half a whole-wheat pita

Feta cheese, tomatoes, kalamata olives,

and lettuce sprinkled with olive oil

Middle Eastern fresh figs

* Azim bread resembles a large, flat biscuit or a tortilla
about 20 cm (8 in) in diameter. You can find them in supermarkets,
natural-foods stores, and Middle Eastern grocery stores.

Mediterranean-style lentil salad
Makes 4 servings

500 ml (2 cups) chicken or vegetable broth

250 ml (1 cup) dried green or brown lentils, rinsed

180 ml (3/4 cup) green onions, chopped

1 red bell pepper, diced

125 ml (1/2 cup) Italian parsley, chopped

125 ml (1/2 cup) walnuts, coarsely chopped

A few leaves of arugula, romaine lettuce, or dandelion greens

Vinaigrette

15 ml (1 tbsp) Dijon mustard

60 ml (1/4 cup) extra-virgin olive oil

45 ml (3 tbsp) red wine vinegar

Salt and pepper to taste

Bring the broth to a boil, add the lentils, lower the heat, cover, and cook over low heat 20 to 25 minutes or until the lentils are tender but not falling apart.

Drain the cooked lentils, then mix them with the other ingredients except the salad greens.

Make the dressing and add to the lentil salad. Serve over the arugula or other greens.

NUTRITIONAL VALUE PER SERVING	
Calories	435
Protein	21 g
Total fat	26 g
Monounsaturated fat	12.4 g
Polyunsaturated fat	7.7 g
Saturated fat	2.7 g
Fibre	9 g
Calcium	76 mg
Iron	6.4 mg
Magnesium	99 mg
Potassium	765 mg
Folic acid	287 mcg
Vitamin C	58 mg

8

Vegetarianism and Its Health Benefits

Vegetarianism and heart disease

Heart disease — including angina, heart failure, infarctus (heart attack), and arteriosclerosis — is the main cause of death among men over fifty and women over seventy-five. In Canada, 37 percent of all deaths are related to such problems.

If you have a family history of heart disease or already have a heart condition, part-time or full-time vegetarianism can be the right approach for you, as there is increasing evidence of its preventive powers. British and American researchers compared the death rate from heart disease among vegetarians and non-vegetarians in a population of 76,000 men and women. They noted that a vegetarian diet could decrease death from heart attack by 24 percent over all. When they looked at the discrepancy between different types of vegetarianism, they found that fish eaters and lacto-ovo-vegetarians were the best off, with a 34 percent lower rate, while strict vegetarians had a rate 26 percent lower and occasional meat eaters had a rate 20 percent lower than that of the general population.

The link between diet and heart disease attracted interest way back in the 1960s, when Dr. Ancel Keys of the University of Minnesota conducted a comparative study of seven countries around the world. He discovered that the eating habits of people on the island of Crete and in Japan were associated with a lower incidence of heart attacks. His observations led to an explosion of research and, in 1994, to the concept of the traditional Mediterranean diet, composed mainly of whole grains, legumes, vegetables, fruits, nuts, olive oil, and fish. This diet — high in fibre, antioxidants, monounsaturated fats, and omega-3 fatty acids, but low in saturated and hydrogenated fats — is quite similar to our part-time vegetarian approach.

In the late 1980s, Dr. Dean Ornish of San Francisco demonstrated that a strict low-fat vegetarian diet, in association with physical activity and meditation, could help patients with major heart problems. Dr. Ornish took photographs inside the arteries of his patients (a procedure called angiography) before and after twelve months of his treatment; his results proved that diet and lifestyle could not only slow down the progression of heart disease but even reduce plaque in the arteries without surgery.

In the mid-1990s, Dr. Serge Renaud and Dr. Michel de Lorgeril also became interested in a diet to reduce mortality among individuals who had already suffered heart attacks. Their Mediterranean-style diet, summarized in the "Lyon Diet Study," is not low in fat, but it is rich in plant foods and omega-3s. After a couple of years on the diet, the mortality rate among vulnerable individuals dropped by 70 percent, an unprecedented result. The classic dietetic approach, which, since the 1960s, aimed at lowering cholesterol by cutting out offending foods, is no longer credible. The new approach aims at adding protective foods, most of them plant foods. This is a great achievement, and that is why the Lyon Diet is regarded as historic!

As a result, the most recent guidelines of the American Heart Association, published in November 2000, have also changed their emphasis: instead of defining precise amounts of fat, they outline what types of fat to keep in the diet, and give top billing to protective foods, including many plant foods. The shopping list has become more appetizing than ever!

Good fat: the heart of the matter

Contrary to a long-standing myth, not all fat is bad for the arteries, and a low-fat diet is not the best way to prevent heart disease. The best strategy is to emphasize good fat.

A vegetarian diet isn't fat-free, and it doesn't necessarily always include good fat. If your menu is full of fried or cheese-based dishes, your arteries won't stay clean. But if you replace meat with legumes or soy products, use olive or canola oil instead of butter, and eat nuts instead of cookies, the quality of the fat you eat will be much healthier.

Olive, canola, and hazelnut oil, filberts, avocados, almonds, pistachio nuts, and olives are good sources of **monounsaturated** fat, which protects the heart. These good fats help to lower LDLs — the bad cholesterol — and tend to increase HDLs — the good cholesterol.

Fatty fish — sardines, mackerel, Atlantic and Pacific salmon, and sea trout — and some micro-algae contain **omega-3s**, which are also good fats, and these foods can fit in with a part-time vegetarian diet. In addition, omega-3s can prevent the blood platelets from clumping and can reduce triglycerides, problems with arrhythmia, and risk of sudden death. That is why the American Heart Association recommends two meals or more of fatty fish per week.

Other fats in the omega-3 family are present in plant foods, such as flaxseeds, walnuts, flaxseed and canola oil, soy, and soy products. Strict vegetarians who never eat fish must rely on these foods to get their fill of omega-3s, while part-time vegetarians and lacto-ovo-vegetarians have a wider variety of foods rich in omega-3s to choose from.

For good heart protection, 3 to 4 grams of omega-3s per day seems an ideal intake. (See table below.)

19. FOODS HIGH IN OMEGA-3s

The amount given is a portion of 100 g (3 1/2 oz).
Values are given in grams.

Sardines	3.3
Mackerel	2.5
Chinook salmon	1.5
Tuna	1.5
Shrimps	0.5
Crab	0.4
Lobster	0.2

19. FOODS HIGH IN OMEGA-3s (cont.)

The amount given is 15 ml (1 tbsp), unless otherwise indicated.

Flaxseed oil	7.5
Flaxseeds	1.9
Canola oil	1.5
Soy oil	0.9
Two omega-3 eggs*	0.5
Walnuts	0.4

* These eggs can be found in the supermarket. They are produced by hens that are fed flax-seeds, and are high in omega-3s.

Foods rich in soluble and insoluble fibre

Vegetarianism involves eating more plant foods — vegetables, fruits, legumes, whole grains, nuts, and seeds — high in soluble and insoluble fibre.

Barley, oats, oat bran, psyllium, flaxseeds, legumes, apples, oranges, grapefruits, and artichokes contain soluble fibre, which plays an important role in the prevention of heart disease by lowering blood cholesterol. The higher the cholesterol, the more effective these fibres are. In fact, among people whose cholesterol is very high, each gram of soluble fibre added to the daily menu can lower the LDLs — bad cholesterol — by 2.2 mg/dL.

Whole grains and whole-grain cereal products are good sources of insoluble fibre, and they also contain large amounts of antioxidants that have been shown to protect both men and women against heart attacks and other heart problems. Refined cereal products have lost all their fibre and antioxidants and do not possess the same protective power (see Table 16, pp. 54–55).

> *When you eat at least 5 servings of fruit and vegetables, some legumes, and whole-grain cereal products — bread, cereals, brown rice, barley, quinoa, and whole-grain pasta — it is easy to reach the goal of at least 25 grams of soluble and insoluble fibre per day.*

• • •

Nuts

You probably think that nuts are full of fat and that they should be enjoyed only as an occasional treat. Well, you're on the wrong track. The good news is that nuts such as almonds, peanuts, pistachios, and pecans are filled with fat that is excellent for the heart, mostly monounsaturated fat, while walnuts also contain more of the omega-3s, another good fat for the heart. All nuts are nutritional powerhouses, providing nutrients that are heart-healthy, such as arginine, fibre (25 percent of which is soluble), vitamin E, folic acid, copper, and magnesium.

Regular consumption of nuts is associated with a lower risk of heart attack among both non-vegetarians and vegetarians. A study carried out among 86,000 nurses showed that those who ate at least 150 g (about 5 oz) of nuts per week had a lower risk of heart problems, compared to those who ate none or just a few nuts — in fact, nuts dropped the risk by 35 percent.

Nuts belong in a healthy diet. They make a much better snack than cookies and chips, which are loaded with hydrogenated fat.

• • •

Lentils and other foods rich in B vitamins

When your diet lacks folic acid and two other B vitamins — vitamin B_6 and vitamin B_{12} — your arteries can be affected. It has been shown that such a deficiency leads to an excess level of homocysteine in the blood, a substance that causes damage to the walls of the blood vessels and can block the arteries. In fact, an additional 5 micromoles of homocysteine in the blood has the same impact as an extra 20 mg of cholesterol, and homocysteine is now considered another major risk factor for heart disease. In order to keep homocysteine levels under the dangerous threshold of 11 micromoles/litre and to protect the cardiovascular system, one must maintain a diet rich in B vitamins.

Lentils are an excellent source of folic acid, while asparagus, avocados, oranges, and leafy green vegetables also contain good amounts. Bananas, nuts, and whole-grain cereals contain large amounts of vitamin B_6. All these foods belong in a vegetarian diet, whether full-time or part-time. Vitamin B_{12}, however, is not found in plant foods, but only in foods of animal origin, such as milk, yogurt, eggs, and cheese. It's easy to get enough of these three vitamins in a part-time vegetarian diet.

Soy and soy products

Tofu, roasted soybeans, soy beverages, and cooked soybeans are all foods rich in soy protein, which has been shown to reduce the risk of heart disease.

In 1995, the *New England Journal of Medicine* reviewed thirty-eight clinical studies that used soy protein to lower cholesterol. The results surprised the scientific community: it was found that soy can reduce LDL (bad) cholesterol and triglycerides without lowering HDL (good) cholesterol. The higher the cholesterol, the more effective soy can be. In October 1999, based on this scientific evidence, the U. S. Food and Drug Administration allowed products containing 6.25 grams of soy protein per serving to carry a label saying that the equivalent of 25 grams of soy protein per day can help to reduce the risk of heart disease.

Soy and its components not only act on cholesterol, they also maintain the elasticity of the artery walls and limit the oxidation of cholesterol. With its high content of arginine — an amino acid — soy promotes the production of nitric acid, which acts like nitroglycerin, a medication prescribed for heart patients that inhibits platelets from sticking to the arterial wall.

20. SOY PROTEINS		
Food	**Quantity**	**Soy protein (g)**
Soy beverage	250 ml (1 cup)	10
Roasted soybeans	60 ml (1/4 cup)	20
Tempeh	125 ml (1/2 cup)	19
Cooked soybeans	125 ml (1/2 cup)	16
Regular tofu	115 g (4 oz)	13
Silken tofu	115 g (4 oz)	9
Soy burger	1	10 to 12
Soy-based cereals	30 g (2/3 cup)	4 to 6

Foods rich in antioxidants

Fresh fruits, very green vegetables, whole grains, soy, and soy products are packed with antioxidants such as carotenoids, vitamin C, vitamin E, zinc, and flavonoids. Antioxidants are chemicals found naturally in foods that have the power to protect vulnerable human tissues and most fats we eat. In this capacity, they protect the cardiovascular system. Two long-term studies followed 75,000 women over four-teen years and 38,000 men over eight years and showed that people who eat a large quantity — more than five servings per day — of citrus fruits, leafy green vegetables, and cruciferous vegetables had 30 percent less risk of suffering a heart attack than people who ate fewer fruits and vegetables.

21. FOODS RICH IN ANTIOXIDANTS

Food	Quantity	Antioxidant units
Prunes	125 ml (1/2 cup)	5,770
Blueberries	180 ml (3/4 cup)	2,400
Kale	375 ml (1 1/2 cups)	1,770
Spinach	750 ml (3 cups)	1,260
Brussels sprouts	250 ml (1 cup)	980
Plums	1 1/2 fruits	949
Broccoli	250 ml (1 cup)	890
Beets	180 ml (3/4 cup)	840
Oranges	1 1/2 fruits	750
Red grapes	250 ml (1 cup)	739
Pink grapefruit	1/2 fruit	748
Red bell peppers	180 ml (3/4 cup)	710

A part-time vegetarian diet can prevent heart disease,
especially if it includes soy and other antioxidants on a regular basis.
• • •

Vegetarianism and diabetes
Diabetes is basically a problem of glucose distribution that arises when the pancreas stops producing, or does not produce enough, insulin. When glucose cannot reach all the cells in the body, it accumulates in the blood and leads to many short- and long-term problems.

Currently, 1.5 million Canadians suffer from diabetes, a disease that can be treat-ed with an appropriate diet, whether they have Type 1 (requiring insulin injections) or Type 2 (most often treated with diet and other medications when needed). According to researchers at the Harvard Medical School, 80 percent of Type 2 diabetics are overweight and have excessive abdominal fat; these diabetics have a risk of developing heart disease three to four times greater than that of the general population, especially if they have high cholesterol. In fact, Type 2 diabetics very often have high triglycerides and low levels of HDL (good) cholesterol. This suggests that diabetics have no choice: they must improve their diet in order to lose weight, achieve a normal cholesterol level, and maintain control of their blood-sugar levels.

On a global level, the lowest incidence of diabetes is found among populations who eat a mostly vegetarian diet. A study among Seventh-Day Adventists, one of the largest groups of vegetarians in the world, showed that vegetarians aged fifty to sixty-nine had a 76 percent lower risk of becoming diabetic than non-vegetarians. A diet richer in plant foods helps to prevent and retards complications of diabetes, such as heart disease and renal, neurological, and visual problems.

Foods rich in carbohydrates

You don't need to avoid all carbohydrates if you have diabetes. Actually, a good diabetic diet should contain a fair amount of carbohydrates (more than 50 percent of daily calories), according to official recommendations issued by the Canadian Diabetes Association and other groups. This doesn't mean splurging on sweets or eating just any food rich in carbohydrates. What it does mean is eating carbohydrates that are rich in fibre, such as legumes, whole-grain cereals, whole-grain pastas, fruits, and vegetables, since these foods encourage better circulation of blood and glucose. Among the carbohydrates that should be avoided or eaten sparingly are refined foods — such as white bread and white rice — sweets, and desserts.

If you have diabetes, you'll have no problem with a vegetarian diet if you eat foods rich in carbohydrates and fibre. However, you must distribute the carbohydrates throughout the day so that your blood-sugar level is maintained at a normal level.

On the other hand, if you are seriously overweight and have high triglycerides and low HDL (good) cholesterol, you are probably insulin-resistant and more vulnerable to heart problems. In this case, you can continue to eat moderate amounts of foods rich in carbohydrates and fibre, but you must limit foods rich in saturated fats, such as meat, processed meats, cheese, and cream. You should give priority in your diet to the monounsaturated fats contained in nuts, olive oil, and avocados, and to the omega-3s contained in fish and flaxseeds. This is completely compatible with part-time vegetarianism. Above all, don't forget about regular physical activity, which helps to lower insulin resistance.

The glycemic index

We cannot ignore the issue of the glycemic index, which is a way of classifying foods rich in carbohydrates. It received widespread attention when actress Suzanne Somers hit the airwaves promoting her carbohydrate-based diet program. In fact, the glycemic index predicts the effects of specific foods on blood-sugar levels. If a food causes a rapid rise in blood sugar, it has a high glycemic index and requires insulin rapidly. If, on the other hand, the food breaks down slowly and releases glucose gradually into the bloodstream, it has a low glycemic index and requires insulin less rapidly. An internationally respected researcher in this area is Professor David Jenkins of the University of Toronto. Dr. Jenkins looked at the impact of foods with a low glycemic index on people with diabetes and noted that these foods led to a better control of blood sugar, lowered insulin resistance, and lowered triglycerides. Legumes, nuts, most vegetables, and certain whole grains — the basic foods of a healthy vegetarian diet — have a low glycemic index.

The glycemic index has some limitations, since the index of a meal does not necessarily equal the sum of the indexes of the foods included in it. To add to the difficulty, different tables of glycemic indexes show conflicting values. This is why we have not included a table of glycemic indexes.

Foods rich in soluble and insoluble fibre

A vegetarian diet usually provides good quantities of dietary fibre, both soluble and insoluble. These two types of fibre are not digested but are very useful for people with diabetes. They each have their own way of working in the body (see Table 22, p. 152).

Soluble fibre retards the absorption of glucose in the colon and improves blood-sugar control. It can even reduce cholesterol. To increase your intake of soluble fibre, add a serving of legumes to your daily menu, replace wheat cereals with oat-bran cereals, replace rice with pot barley, eat more berries, and you've got it made!

Insoluble fibre absorbs a lot of water, creates greater food volume, and reduces transit time in the gut; by doing so, it improves the bacterial flora, protects the colon's lining, and increases the volume of feces. It definitely prevents constipation.

The American Diabetes Association recommends that about 40 grams of soluble and insoluble fibre be consumed per day, which is compatible with a vegetarian diet. Since fibre is found only in plant foods, the more plant foods in the menu, the more fibre you eat. But do not increase your fibre intake too rapidly. Do it gradually, and be sure to drink more water. Otherwise, you might end up feeling bloated or uncomfortable.

Foods rich in fibre offer other health-promoting compounds not found in refined foods, such as greater amounts of magnesium and chromium, two minerals that work closely with insulin. These foods are usually low in fat, and at the same time they increase your feeling of fullness — two factors that can help you to achieve or maintain a healthy weight.

22. THE MAIN SOURCES OF SOLUBLE AND INSOLUBLE FIBRE

Soluble fibre	Insoluble fibre
Oat bran and corn bran	Wheat bran
Rolled oats	Wheat-bran cereals
Legumes	Whole grains
Barley and rye	Nuts
Apples, plums, and small berries	Sunflower seeds
Flaxseeds	Flaxseeds
Vegetables	Fruits and vegetables

Different fats and their functions

Not all fats work the same way, and when diabetes is a problem, good fats become very important.

A number of studies have shown that a diet rich in monounsaturated fat can lower triglycerides, improve blood-sugar control, and reduce insulin resistance. Olive, canola, and hazelnut oils, olives, avocados, almonds, pistachios, hazelnuts, and peanuts are all good sources of monounsaturated fats that can also help lower LDL cholesterol without affecting the good HDL cholesterol. Snacking on almonds instead of cookies and using olive-oil dressings on your salads is an easy way to increase your intake of this type of fat.

Omega-3s — present in fatty fish, flaxseeds, soy, and soy products — also have the power to drive down triglycerides. In addition, they have anti-clotting and anti-inflammatory effects. In a part-time vegetarian approach, a few fish meals per week can improve a heart condition.

The fats that should be restricted are the saturated fats in meats and cheeses, as well as trans-fats hidden in bakery products, fried foods, and all products with hydrogenated fats.

The rule of three "real meals" a day

If you have diabetes, it is vital for you to adopt a regular eating schedule that translates into three "real meals" a day, plus snacks when needed. "Real meals" must contain an adequate amount of protein and fibre, to stabilize blood-sugar levels. If these meals are vegetarian, they should be planned around legumes or soy and served with vegetables, whole grains, and fruit. If these meals include fish, you get protein with a dose of omega-3s. "Real meals" are essential to proper blood-sugar control.

23. A FEW IDEAS FOR "REAL MEALS"

Spinach salad with olive-oil dressing
Chickpea stew
Pot barley
Mango and yogurt smoothie

Grated carrot salad
Sautéed tofu on green vegetables
Oat-bran bread
Kiwi fruit or cantaloupe

Raw vegetables with yogurt dip
Lentil salad with goat cheese
Whole-wheat pita
Apple or pear sauce

Tomato juice
Shrimp salad on half an avocado
Dark rye bread
Clementines or orange sections

Exercise

Whatever you choose to eat, regular activity really helps control your diabetes. If you have Type 2 diabetes, regular exercise enables all the cells in your body to use the insulin that you produce and helps to stimulate your metabolism so that you burn calories more efficiently.

If you receive insulin injections, exercise can still help. However, you may need to make certain adjustments concerning your intake of foods before, during, and after exercise to prevent low blood sugar.

Part-time vegetarianism is a good way to make the transition to a diet richer in plant foods without upsetting the blood-sugar levels. If you have just found out that you have diabetes, or if you are pregnant and have diabetes, a professional dietitian can help you adjust a vegetarian diet to your needs.

• • •

Vegetarianism and cancer

Cancer has become less deadly, thanks to early diagnosis and more effective treatments, but it is still the leading cause of death among women under the age of seventy-four. Some preventive measures exist, but are they well enough known? In 1997, the World Cancer Research Fund and the American Institute for Cancer Research published a major report, *Diet, Nutrition, and Cancer Prevention: A Global Perspective*, which took into account more than 4,500 studies that had been carefully reviewed by experts. It reported that lacto-ovo-vegetarians around the world (such as the Seventh-Day Adventists) died less often from cancer than did the general population. The difference was sometimes as much as 70 percent. (It should be noted that Seventh-Day Adventists do not smoke or consume alcohol or caffeine.) In a population of 2,000 German vegetarians followed for almost eleven years, the mortality rate linked to cancer was 48 percent lower among men and 74 percent lower among women than in the general population. Similar differences were reported among other vegetarian groups in England and the United States, and so vegetarianism seems to have some preventive value when it comes to cancer. The benefits observed among vegetarians also exist among semi-vegetarian groups.

These experts found convincing evidence linking the preventive effect of fruits and vegetables against cancers of the mouth and pharynx, esophagus, lungs, stomach, colon, and rectum. For cancer of the larynx, pancreas, breast, and bladder, the evidence seems probable, and for other cancers, the link is possible.

The report concludes with a list of recommended dietary habits to reduce the risk of cancer. Three recommendations are devoted to plant foods:

- Adopt a plant-based diet, high in a variety of vegetables, fruits, legumes, and minimally processed starches.
- Eat five to ten servings of a variety of fruits and vegetables per day throughout the year.
- Eat more than seven servings per day of a variety of whole grains, legumes, and tuberous and root vegetables.

Some researchers have been suggesting a diet rich in fruits and vegetables to help reduce the risk of cancer since 1933!

Cancer and plant foods

When we were studying to become dietitians in the 1960s, we learned about vitamins, minerals, and cellulose in plant foods. The scientific data stopped there, more or less . . . Since then, researchers have identified hundreds, maybe thousands, of natural chemicals in plant foods that seem to have preventive powers. So fruits, vegetables, cereals, nuts, and legumes have become superstars.

For instance, vitamins C, E, and beta carotene have acquired the status of antioxidants. Well-known minerals, such as iron and calcium, have been joined by other important micronutrients such as selenium, zinc, manganese, copper, chromium, and boron, and all these are present in plant foods. Cellulose, which went almost unnoticed in our nutrition books, has given way to the famous family of dietary fibres, soluble and insoluble, each with a specific effect.

Recently, there has been discussion concerning resistant starches. These starches are not digested, but they leave traces when they pass through the digestive tract. They stimulate the production of substances that improve the intestinal flora and modify the behaviour of local intestinal carcinogens. Whole grains, legumes, tuberous and root vegetables, and some fruits are rich in both fibre and resistant starches.

Added to this list are phytochemicals that also seem to play a preventive role against cancer. There are dozens of them, including flavonoids, lignans, lycopene, and isoflavones. Most of these compounds are antioxidants that block or inhibit the growth of cancerous cells in different tissues of the body.

Flavonoids

Flavonoids are powerful antioxidants. They neutralize free radicals that are naturally present but can become a nuisance in the human body. Present in many fruits and vegetables, flavonoids protect the cell, as well as proteins and fats, against the damages of oxidation; they inhibit pro-carcinogens and impede development of malignant tumors. Five to ten servings of fresh fruits and vegetables per day ensure an adequate intake of flavonoids.

Lignans

Lignans are substances that resemble the estrogen naturally secreted by the ovaries; they come from plants and are called phytoestrogens. Lignans are absorbed and activated by the intestinal flora. They can reduce the risk of certain cancers, including breast and prostate cancer. How they work is not fully understood, but their anticancer power seems to be associated with their ability to block or limit the circulation of other estrogens.

Oats, rye, and pot barley contain lignans, but flaxseeds provide the richest source.

Professor Lilian Thompson, an internationally known expert from the University of Toronto, conducted a study with women who had breast cancer. Her research showed that a daily dose of 25 grams (40 ml) of flaxseeds integrated in the daily diet before surgery could significantly reduce the growth rate of malignant tumours.

There are studies still in progress, but while we wait for definitive answers, a dose of 10 to 15 grams (15 to 20 ml) of ground flaxseeds per day is considered a good preventive measure.

Lycopene

Lycopene is a member of the carotenoid family, as is betacarotene. It is found mainly in red or pink fruits, such as red tomatoes (raw or cooked), papaya, pink grapefruit, watermelon, and pink guava.

Among all carotenoids, lycopene has the highest antioxidant capacity. People who eat lots of tomatoes have more lycopene in their blood and a lower incidence of cancer, mainly of the prostate, stomach, and lungs. Research has been focused mainly on prostate cancer, the most common cancer among men in North America. In the famous Health Professionals Follow-up Study (HPFS), conducted with 44,000 men, the risk of prostate cancer was lowered by 21 percent among those who ate large quantities of tomatoes. There was also a drop of up to 60 percent among those who had the highest levels of lycopene in the blood.

Consumption of more than 6.4 milligrams of lycopene per day seems to be enough to diminish the risk of prostate cancer.

24. FOODS HIGH IN LYCOPENE

Values are given in milligrams.

Food	Portion	Lycopene
Fresh tomatoes	1 medium fruit	1 to 6
Pizza sauce	63 g (1/4 cup)	8
Cooked tomatoes	126 g (1/2 cup)	5
Tomato sauce	61 g (1/2 cup)	4
Tomato paste	33 g (2 tbsp)	2 to 5
Tomato juice	250 ml (1 cup)	12 to 28
Papaya	1 medium fruit	6 to 16
Pink grapefruit	1/2 fruit	4
Watermelon	160 g (1 cup)	4 to 12

Isoflavones (soy products)

Isoflavones are estrogen-like substances present in soy and soy products; they have a weaker power than estrogen produced by the ovaries (see Table 11, p. 41).

The interest in isoflavones began when researchers noticed that Japanese women who ate soy on a daily basis did not have the same menopausal symptoms as Western women. They looked more closely at the Japanese diet and identified soy as the main source of plant estrogen. They also took note of the low incidence of breast cancer in Japan.

When you hear that soy might increase the risk of breast cancer, consider it a false rumour: no study yet has proven such an allegation. On the contrary, at least ten population studies conducted in the 1990s have pointed to a lower incidence of breast cancer in Asia and linked the higher intake of soy to this reduced risk. Scientists then undertook other studies, some in the lab and some among groups of women.

In the lab, the in vitro studies showed that the isoflavones contained in soy could block the development of breast and prostate cancer cells, whether they were hormone-dependent or not. It was also noted that isoflavones could prevent the propagation of these cancerous cells.

Clinical studies conducted with women have also provided interesting indications concerning the protective effect of soy. Researchers at the University of Minnesota worked with a group of post-menopausal women and looked at how soy affected their hormonal levels. For three periods of three months, women received three different doses of soy protein. The effect of soy on hormones produced by the body was then measured. The authors concluded that intake of soy reduces the proportion of harmful hormones by deactivating them, which would explain in part soy's preventive mechanism against cancer.

In Australia, post-menopausal women diagnosed with breast cancer were compared with healthy women. Women with cancer excreted fewer isoflavones in their urine than did the healthy women. Since urinary excretion of isoflavones is a good indicator of soy intake, and since there were no significant differences among the other indicators measured — fat, carbohydrates, fibre, estrogen, and other hormones — the research tends to confirm the protective effect of soy isoflavones.

The work done on lab animals by Dr. Coral Lamartinière and his team at the University of Alabama suggests that soy intake before puberty may provide a greater protection against development of breast cancer later in life. The earlier the age at which the subject begins to eat soy, the better the protection.

One last study, published in the spring of 2001, tends to demonstrate that soy is far from being harmful for women with breast cancer taking tamoxifen, an anti-cancer medication. The animals in this study — which were receiving both soy and the medication — experienced a 62 percent reduction in the number of tumours, compared to only 29 percent when the tamoxifen was used alone.

It is important to emphasize that research showing the protective effect of soy among women before and after menopause used soy in a food form: soy protein, tofu, or soy beverage. Isoflavone supplements sold in pills or capsules have not been subjected to comparable studies until now.

The file isn't closed, but the positive evidence is accumulating. An intake of 50 milligrams of isoflavones per day can benefit both men and women.

Women who eat a lot of foods rich in isoflavones apparently reduce their risk of endometrial cancer by 54 percent, according to a study published in the *American Journal of Epidemiology.*

Soy intake also protects men. In fact, Asian men have much lower death rates linked to prostate cancer than do men in the United States. Isoflavones seem to inhibit the growth of prostate cancer cells, whether hormone-dependent or not. According to scientists at the University of Alabama in Birmingham, lacto-ovo-vegetarians who drink two glasses of soy beverage per day seem to lower their risk of prostate cancer by 70 percent.

Other substances contained in soy can play a role in reducing cancer risks — phenolic acid, phytic acid, saponines, omega-3 fatty acids — but, for the moment, most studies have been done with isoflavones.

"It is not the meat on the menu that causes problems, but the lack of vegetables, fruits, and other plant foods," stated Charles Elson, a specialist on phytochemicals in plant foods at the University of Wisconsin–Madison, when he was asked whether it was essential to be a strict vegetarian to prevent cancer.

• • •

Vegetarianism and high blood pressure

One Canadian out of five suffers from high blood pressure, and this proportion rises to one out of two after sixty-five years of age. Hypertension is not painful, but it can lead silently to a stroke or kidney disease. The classic way to deal with high blood pressure has been to cut salt, but this method has not been stunningly successful. Other avenues have been explored, such as weight loss, increased physical activity, reduced alcohol consumption, and quitting smoking. These approaches are all very healthy and can reduce the risk of heart disease, but they do not lower blood pressure significantly when they are adopted separately.

The good news is that the Dietary Approaches to Stop Hypertension (DASH) study has shown positive results and can help all those with high blood pressure or those who want to prevent the problem. This study was conducted in 1997 with 459 adults with blood pressures of 160 over 80 to 95. After only two weeks, hypertensive patients following the improved diet experienced a drop in blood pressure comparable to that obtained with medication — a reduction of 11.4 mmHg of systolic pressure and 5.5 mmHg of diastolic pressure.

If you are interested in vegetarianism and have high blood pressure, you will be thrilled to learn the details of this study. The diet prescription consists of eating at least eight to ten servings of fruits and vegetables, two to three servings of low-fat dairy products, and not more than 3,000 mg of sodium (salt) per day. The menu also contains whole grains every day, but little saturated fat, and does not exclude lean meats occasionally, fish, nuts, and unsalted seeds, and a limited quantity of alcohol. With regard to exercise and lifestyle, the prescription is to walk briskly thirty to forty-five minutes five days a week, not to smoke, and to lose 4 to 5 kg (about 10 lb), if needed. This approach brings together most of the winning strategies studied separately and has proven to be more successful.

The innovative aspect of the DASH study is the addition of foods rich in potassium, magnesium, and calcium — the eight to ten servings of fruits and vegetables and two to three servings of low-fat dairy products — to the menu. The important mineral contribution provided by these foods seems to have a favourable effect on blood pressure, especially when combined with a healthy lifestyle.

All of this comes back to a basic fact: a diet high in fibre, potassium, magnesium, and calcium and low in saturated fats and in fats in general, combined with a healthy lifestyle, leads to a lowering of blood pressure among people with hypertension and maintains normal blood pressure in others.

25. DAILY MENU ACCORDING TO THE DASH APPROACH

Morning: Orange, oatmeal, skim milk, and banana

Lunch: Broiled salmon, Swiss chard, butternut squash, brown rice, and cantaloupe

Snack: Skim milk

Supper: Lentil salad, roasted soy nuts, romaine lettuce, bell pepper, whole-wheat bread, plain yogurt, and strawberry coulis

This colourful menu supplies 6,000 mg of potassium, 765 mg of magnesium, and 1,300 mg of calcium, thanks to the four servings of fruits, five servings of vegetables, and three servings of low-fat dairy products.

Lentils alone supply more than 700 mg of potassium, while Swiss chard supplies almost 1,000 mg. Swiss chard, lentils, and whole grains also provide most of the magnesium, and dairy products and Swiss chard supply most of the calcium on the menu.

This type of menu promotes normal blood pressure and general good health.

• • •

Appendix
Supermarket Minute Foods

GM = genetically modified; NGM = non-genetically modified.

Amy's
Vegetable Lasagna

Serving size: 9.5 oz

Protein: 14 g

Ingredients: organic lasagna pasta (organic semolina flour, organic whole wheat durum flour, water), organic tomato purée, organic zucchini, organic spinach, part-skim mozzarella cheese, low fat cottage cheese, organic onions, organic carrots, extra-virgin olive oil, spices, parmesan cheese, grade AA butter, sea salt, garlic (all cheeses are made without animal enzymes or rennet)

Format: frozen

Remarks: all organic, no GM foods

Tofu Vegetable Lasagna

Serving size: 9.5 oz

Protein: 13 g

Ingredients: organic lasagna pasta (organic semolina flour, organic whole wheat durum flour, water), organic tomatoes, onions, filtered water, mozzarella-style soy cheese (fresh soy milk made from organic soy beans and filtered water, soy oil, caseinate-a milk-derived protein, fresh tofu, salt, soy lecithin, natural flavour, natural vegetable gums), organic zucchini, organic tofu, organic spinach, olive oil, organic carrots, spices, sea salt, garlic

Format: frozen

Remarks: all organic, no GM foods

Burritos

Serving size: 6 oz

Protein: 10 g

Ingredients: organic pinto beans, filtered water, organic whole wheat and wheat flour, organic brown rice, organic crushed tomatoes, organic onions, expeller-pressed high oleic safflower oil, cheddar and jack cheeses, organic bell peppers, sweet rice flour, sea salt, spices, garlic (all cheeses are made without animal enzymes or rennet)

Format: frozen

Remarks: all organic, no GM foods

Enchiladas

Serving size: 10 oz

Protein: 7 g

Ingredients: filtered water, organic long grain white rice, organic pinto beans, organic corn tortilla (organic white corn cooked in water with a trace of lime), organic tomatoes, onions, organic bell peppers, organic tofu, organic black beans, expeller-pressed safflower oil, organic zucchini, sweet rice flour, spices, sea salt, tapioca flour, black olives, garlic, green chilies

Format: frozen

Remarks: all organic, no GM foods

Soups (Lentil)

Serving size: 250 ml
Protein: 8 g
Ingredients: filtered water, organic lentils, organic celery, organic onions, organic
               carrots, organic potatoes, organic extra-virgin olive oil, sea salt, spices
Format: canned
Remarks: all organic, no GM foods

Bombay Dine

Seven Bean & Vegetable Soup

Serving size: 245 ml (1 cup)
Protein: 11 g
Ingredients: water, beans (soya, pinto, white, red kidney, chickpeas, green lentils,
               mung), carrots, tomatoes, green peas, green beans, tomato paste, corn,
               celery, sea salt, black pepper, basil, parsley, oregano
Format: canned
Remarks: all organic

White Bean Soup

Serving size: 245 ml (1 cup)
Protein: 9 g
Ingredients: water, white beans, tomatoes, carrots, celery, onions, sea salt, black
               pepper, garlic
Format: canned
Remarks: all organic

Lentil Original

Serving size: 245 ml (1 cup)
Protein: 9 g
Ingredients: water, green lentils, carrots, tomato paste, onions, celery, sea salt, black
               pepper
Format: canned
Remarks: all organic

Cascadian Farm
Moroccan Organic Vegetarian Meal
Serving size: 454 g (16 oz)

Protein: 13 g

Ingredients: bulgur wheat, lentils, garbanzo beans, onions, red peppers, raisins, spices, HI Oleic sunflower oil, sea salt, canola oil, turmeric

Format: frozen

Remarks: all organic

Aztec Organic Vegetarian Meal
Serving size: 454 g (16 oz)

Protein: 12 g

Ingredients: black beans, brown rice, corn, onions, red peppers, wheat berries, spices, HI Oleic sunflower oil, sea salt, dehydrated garlic

Format: frozen

Remarks: all organic

Indian Organic Vegetarian Meal
Serving size: 454 g (16 oz)

Protein: 12 g

Ingredients: basmati rice, garbanzo beans, tomatoes, peas, onion, spices, coconut, sugar, sea salt, HI Oleic sunflower oil, turmeric

Format: frozen

Remarks: all organic

Szechuan Organic Vegetarian Meal
Serving size: 454 g (16 oz)

Protein: 14 g

Ingredients: white basmati rice, broccoli, carrots, black beans, soybeans, peas, toasted sesame oil, black sesame seeds, dried tamari soy sauce, sea salt, spices, dehydrated garlic, rice vinegar, sugar, autolyzed yeast extract, dehydrated red chili, xanthan gum

Format: frozen

Remarks: all organic

Green Cuisine

7-Grain Tempeh

Serving size: 100 g
Protein: 16 g
Ingredients: organic soybeans, brown rice, sunflower seeds, millet, oats, barley, wild rice, spelt, filtered water, culture
Format: frozen
Remarks: all organic, no GM foods

Soybean Tempeh

Serving size: 100 g
Protein: 18 g
Ingredients: organic soybeans, filtered water, culture
Format: frozen
Remarks: all organic, no GM foods

Health Valley

Chili Mild 3-Bean

Serving size: 245 g
Protein: 13 g
Ingredients: filtered water, tomatoes, organic pinto beans, onions, carrots, tomato paste, red kidney beans, soy proteins, small white beans, natural vegetable flavour, green bell peppers, chili pepper, honey, sea salt, unsulfured molasses, garlic powder, cumin, potato flakes, paprika, ground bay leaves, sage, basil, oregano
Format: canned
Remarks: all organic, no GM foods

Chili Spicy Black Bean

Serving size: 245 g

Protein: 13 g

Ingredients: filtered water, organic tomatoes, organic black beans, onions, pinto beans, carrots, tomato paste, soy proteins, green bell peppers, chili pepper, honey, natural vegetable flavour, unsulfured molasses, sea salt, garlic powder, cumin, potato flakes, paprika, ground bay leaves, sage, oregano, basil

Format: canned

Remarks: all organic, no GM foods

5-Bean Vegetable Soup

Serving size: 240 g

Protein: 10 g

Ingredients: filtered water, carrots, organic pinto beans, organic black beans, celery, organic tomatoes, onions, potatoes, tomato paste, kidney beans, honey, lima beans, green beans, cabbage, onion powder, garbanzo beans, natural vegetable broth, natural vegetable flavour, broccoli, cauliflower, sea salt, garlic powder, lemon juice concentrate, green bell peppers, parsley, white pepper, natural beta-carotene, bay leaves, sage, basil, oregano

Format: canned

Remarks: all organic, no GM foods

Chili Mild Black Beans

Serving size: 245 g

Protein: 13 g

Ingredients: filtered water, tomatoes, organic black beans, onions, pinto beans, carrots, tomato paste, soy proteins, honey, green bell peppers, natural vegetable flavour, chili pepper, unsulfured molasses, sea salt, garlic powder, cumin, potato flakes, paprika, ground bay leaves, sage, oregano, basil

Format: canned

Remarks: all organic, no GM foods

Black Bean and Vegetable Soup

Serving size:　240 g

Protein:　11 g

Ingredients:　filtered water, organic black beans, onions, organic tomatoes, tomato paste, carrots, honey, organic corn, celery, small white beans, red bell peppers, natural vegetable broth, natural vegetable flavour, sea salt, potato flakes, lemon juice concentrate, garlic powder, cilantro, onion powder, white pepper, bay leaves, basil, natural beta-carotene, parsley, sage, oregano

Format:　canned

Remarks:　all organic, no GM foods

Lightlife

Chick'n Strips

Serving size:　85 g

Protein:　14 g

Ingredients:　water, textured soy protein concentrate, natural flavours, salt, yeast extract, potassium chloride, chicory fibre, natural smoke flavour, vitamins and minerals

Format:　refrigerated

Remarks:　steak strips also available

Seasoned Chick'n

Serving size:　113 g

Protein:　26g

Ingredients:　water, soy protein isolate, textured wheat gluten, soybeans, maltodextrin, yeast extract, natural flavours, potassium chloride, salt, soy oil, dipotassium phosphate, barley malt, onion, garlic, dextrose, paprika, white pepper, annato, turmeric, vitamins and minerals

Format:　refrigerated

Remarks:　Salisbury steak in mushroom sauce also available

Momo's Veggie Kitchen
Mo' Beef Veggie Burger
Serving size: 85 g

Protein: 19.2 g

Ingredients: water, NGM soy protein concentrate, NGM sunflower oil, whey protein, soy protein isolate, textured soy protein, evaporated cane juice, glucose, salt, black pepper, glycine, vitamins and minerals

Format: frozen

Remarks: no GM foods

Mo' Chicken Veggie Burger
Serving size: 85 g

Protein: 18 g

Ingredients: water, NGM soy protein concentrate, NGM sunflower oil, whey protein, soy protein isolate, textured soy protein, evaporated cane juice, glucose, salt, black pepper, glycine, vitamins and minerals

Format: frozen

Remarks: no GM foods

Mo' Tuna Veggie Filets
Serving size: 85 g

Protein: 16 g

Ingredients: water, NGM soy protein concentrate, NGM sunflower oil, wheat gluten, glucose, evaporated cane juice, salt, seasoning, natural flavours, dill weed, lemon oil, natural food colour

Format: frozen

Remarks: no GM foods

Natural Choice
Italian Bean Dish

Serving size:	425 g (13 oz)
Protein:	nutritional information not available
Ingredients:	baby lima beans, filtered water, diced tomatoes, zucchini, onions, cannellini beans, spinach, potato flakes, textured soy protein, chickpea flour, olive oil, garlic, sea salt, herbs and spices
Format:	canned
Remarks:	all organic, no GM foods

3-Bean Chili

Serving Size:	425 g (13 oz)
Protein:	nutritional information not available
Ingredients:	filtered water, tomatoes, pinto beans, kidney beans, black beans, tomato paste, textured soy protein, onions, yellow corn, chili pepper powder, onion powder, marsala wine, sea salt, cane sugar, herbs and spices
Format:	canned
Remarks:	all organic, no GM foods

Asian Bean Dish

Serving size:	425 g (13 oz)
Protein:	nutritional information not available
Ingredients:	filtered water, soy beans, yams, adzuki beans, onion, turnips, daikon, miso, arame, potato flakes, mirin, sea salt, garlic powder, black pepper
Format:	canned
Remarks:	all organic, no GM foods

Mediterranean Bean Dish

Serving size:	425 g (13 oz)
Protein:	nutritional information not available
Ingredients:	filtered water, garbanzo beans, diced tomatoes, celery, onions, chickpea flour, olive oil, potato flakes, garlic, lemon juice, sea salt, herbs and spices
Format:	canned
Remarks:	all organic, no GM foods

Nutty Island Foods

Isadora's Go-Nuts Burger

Serving size: 85 g

Protein: 12.5 g

Ingredients: walnuts, eggs, bread crumbs, carrots, onion, Monterey Jack cheese, canola oil, sunflower seeds, tamari soy sauce, garlic, spices

Format: frozen

President's Choice

Chickenless Kiev

Serving size: 114 g

Protein: 20 g

Ingredients: water, sunflower oil, cream cheese, soy protein isolate + textured soy protein, breadcrumbs, wheat gluten, dried egg white, butter, yeast, natural and artificial flavours, garlic powder, sea salt, potato starch, wheat flour, spices, vitamins and minerals, thickeners

Format: frozen

Chickenless Drumsticks

Serving size: 120 g

Protein: 23 g

Ingredients: water, sunflower oil, soy protein isolate + textured soy protein, bread crumbs, wheat gluten, dried egg white, yeast, wheat germ, onion powder, tomato paste, sugar, white vinegar, natural and artificial flavours, garlic powder, sea salt, potato starch, wheat flour, spices, vitamins and minerals, thickeners

Format: frozen

President's Choice "Too Good to Be True"

Southwestern 5-Bean Instant soup

Serving size: 68 g dry weight (makes about 250ml/1 cup)

Protein: 13 g

Ingredients: precooked beans, dehydrated vegetables, precooked lentils, brown rice, syrup powder, dried yeast, spices, salt, paprika, soy sauce powder, yeast extract, natural flavours

Format: dehydrated

Remarks: add hot water

Minestrone and Pasta Instant Soup

Serving size: 66 g dry weight (makes about 250 ml/1 cup)

Protein: 11 g

Ingredients: ribbon pasta, dehydrated vegetables, textured vegetable protein, Parmesan cheese, maltodextrin, brown sugar, soy sauce powder, corn flour, spices, salt, vinegar powder, guar gum, xanthan gum

Format: dehydrated

Remarks: add hot water

Vegetable Couscous Instant Soup

Serving size: 56 g dry weight (makes about 1 cup)

Protein: 9 g

Ingredients: precooked couscous, dehydrated vegetables, precooked beans, precooked lentils, dried yeast, miso powder, salt, natural flavours, spices, maltodextrin, Parmesan cheese, vinegar powder, yeast extract

Format: dehydrated

Remarks: add hot water

Vegetarian 3-Bean Chili

Serving size: 295 g

Protein: 14 g

Ingredients: tomato sauce, water, kidney beans, onion, celery, tomato paste, pinto beans, black turtle beans, soy sauce, textured vegetable protein, sugar, chili powder, olive oil, garlic, onion powder, concentrated lemon juice, modified cornstarch, salt, spices, dehydrated parsley

Format: frozen

Cheese and Spinach Cannelloni

Serving size: 259 g

Protein: 16 g

Ingredients: pasta: water, durum wheat semolina, frozen whole eggs; sauce: tomato sauce, water, tomato paste, onion, modified cornstarch, sugar, green olives, garlic, parsley, canola oil, salt, spices; filling: cottage cheese, ricotta cheese, spinach, tofu preparation, modified cornstarch, salt, sun-dried tomatoes, dehydrated onions, concentrated lemon juice, garlic powder, spices

Format: frozen

Vegetable Quesadilla

Serving size: 125 g

Protein: 14 g

Ingredients: tortilla: whole-wheat flour, enriched white flour, canola oil shortening, baking powder, salt, preservatives, skim milk powder; filling: Monterey Jack cheese, green tomatoes, green bell peppers, water, onion, black beans, corn, red bell peppers, red and green jalapeño peppers, canola oil, modified cornstarch, salt, seasonings

Format: frozen

Primo

Lentil Hearty Soup

Serving size: 250 ml (1 cup)

Protein: 9.8 g

Ingredients: water, lentils, celery, spinach, tomato paste, salt, dehydrated onions, vegetable oil, spice

Format: canned

Seapoint Farm

Edamame Soybean Rice Bowl: Vegetable Fried Rice

Serving size: 340 g

Protein: 18 g

Ingredients: seasoned rice, edamame (soybeans), vegetable blend (carrots, onions, corn), ginger garlic sauce

Format: frozen

Remarks: no GM foods

Edamame Soybean Rice Bowl: Teriyaki Vegetable

Serving size: 340 g

Protein: 16 g

Ingredients: cooked rice, edamame (soybeans), teriyaki sauce, vegetable blend (corn, carrots, red bell peppers)

Format: frozen

Remarks: no GM foods

Edamame Soybean Rice Bowl: Kung Pao Vegetable

Serving size: 340 g

Protein: 17 g

Ingredients: cooked rice, edamame (soybeans), kung pao sauce, vegetable blend (carrots, bell peppers, bamboo shoots), dry roasted peanuts

Format: frozen

Remarks: no GM foods

Edamame Soybean Rice Bowl: Szechuan Vegetable

Serving size: 340 g

Protein: 15 g

Ingredients: cooked rice, edamame (soybeans), Szechuan sauce, vegetable blend (carrots, red bell peppers, broccoli)

Format: frozen

Remarks: no GM foods

Second Nature
Spicy Bean Burger
Serving size: 91 g
Protein: 13 g
Ingredients: water, soy protein concentrate, black beans, organic sweet corn, spices, sunflower oil, cellulose gum, salt
Format: frozen
Remarks: all organic, no GM foods, microwaveable

Vegetable Burger
Serving size: 91 g
Protein: 13 g
Ingredients: water, organic vegetables (sweet corn, peas, green beans, broccoli, cauliflower, dry roasted onion), soy protein concentrate, spices, sunflower oil, cellulose gum, salt
Format: frozen
Remarks: all organic, no GM foods, microwaveable

Meatless Burger
Serving size: 91 g
Protein: 15 g
Ingredients: water, soy protein concentrate, sunflower oil, dehydrated onion, cellulose gum, organic lemon juice, salt, tomato powder, garlic, spices, malt
Format: frozen
Remarks: all organic, no GM foods, microwaveable

Shari Ann's
Organic Veggie Chili
Serving size: 250 g (1 cup)
Protein: 10 g
Ingredients: water, pinto beans, tomato purée, kamut grain, onions, brown rice flour, jalapeños, sea salt, honey, spices
Format: canned
Remarks: all organic, no GM foods

Spicy Veggie Chili

Serving size:	250 g (1 cup)
Protein:	10 g
Ingredients:	water, pinto beans, tomato purée, kamut grain, onions, brown rice flour, jalapeños, sea salt, honey, spices
Format:	canned
Remarks:	all organic, no GM foods

Italian-Style White Bean Soup

Serving size:	250 g (1 cup)
Protein:	10 g
Ingredients:	water, navy beans, carrots, celery, onion, vegetarian Worcestershire sauce (apple cider vinegar, molasses, honey, soy sauce, tamarind, onion, garlic, shallots, spices), sea salt, brown rice flour, spices, Tabasco (vinegar, red peppers, salt)
Format:	canned
Remarks:	all organic, no GM foods

French-Style Green Lentil Soup

Serving size:	252 g (1 cup)
Protein:	10 g
Ingredients:	water, French green lentils, onion, certified organic brown rice flour, tamari (water, soybeans, sea salt), carrots, celery, spices
Format:	canned
Remarks:	all organic, no GM foods

Organic Spicy Mexican Bean Soup

Serving size:	250 g (1 cup)
Protein:	10 g
Ingredients:	water, certified organic chili and/or pinto beans, certified organic black beans, certified organic cider vinegar, certified organic brown rice flour, certified organic onion, jalapeño pepper, lime juice, sea salt, spices
Format:	canned
Remarks:	all organic, no GM foods

Split Pea Soup

Serving size: 250 g (1 cup)

Protein: 10 g

Ingredients: water, split peas, onion, carrots, celery, brown rice flour, vegetarian Worcestershire sauce, spices, sea salt

Format: canned

Remarks: all organic, no GM foods

Soyganic
Baked Tofu in Blocks (Italian, Szechuan, Teriyaki)

Serving size: 100 g

Protein: 12 g

Ingredients: organically grown soybeans, teriyaki, Szechuan, or Italian sauce, calcium sulphate

Format: refrigerated

Remarks: all organic

Taste Adventure
Black Bean Soup

Serving size: 65 g

Protein: 13 g

Ingredients: precooked black beans, sea salt, red chili peppers, garlic, basil, oregano, thyme, rosemary, rice vinegar

Format: boxed

Minestrone Soup

Serving size: 65 g

Protein: 9 g

Ingredients: precooked beans (white, red and pinto beans), whole-wheat pasta, precooked lentils, tomatoes, brown rice, carrots, herbs, spices, green beans, peas, salt, onions, garlic

Format: boxed

Turtle Island Foods

Tofurky Drummettes

Serving size: 85 g

Protein: 11 g

Ingredients: textured soy protein, soy tempeh (NGM soybeans grown without chemical fertilizers, pesticides or herbicides, water, apple cider vinegar, starter culture), grated carrots, wild rice, natural cane sweetener, natural vegetarian flavour, dried cranberries, soy sauce, soy protein isolate, carrageenan (from seaweed), herbs and spices

Format: frozen

Remarks: no GM foods

Stuffed Tofu Roast

Serving size: 114 g

Protein: 26 g

Ingredients: tofu roast: water, vital wheat gluten, tofu (water, NGM soybeans grown without chemical fertilizers, pesticides or herbicides), white beans, garbanzo beans, natural vegetarian flavour, cold-pressed canola oil, tamari, spices, lemon juice, calcium lactate from beets, salt; stuffing: brown rice, wild rice, bread cubes, onion, celery, natural vegetarian seasoning, cold-pressed canola oil, herbs and spices

Format: frozen

Remarks: no GM foods

Tofurky Deli Slices (Original, Hickory Smoked)

Serving size: 43 g

Protein: 13 g

Ingredients: water, vital wheat gluten, tofu, white beans, garbanzo beans, natural vegetarian flavour, cold-pressed canola oil, shoyu, spices, lemon juice, calcium lactate from beets, salt

Format: frozen or refrigerated

Veat All Natural
Chick'n Free Nuggets
Serving size: 70 g

Protein: 14 g

Ingredients: water, texturized vegetarian protein, canola oil, soy protein, whey protein, wheat protein, sodium caseinate, sugar, wheat starch, sea salt, tamarind powder, yeast extract, spices, natural flavour

Format: frozen

Remarks: no GM foods

Woodstock Organics
Lentil Soup with Carrots
Serving size: 213 g

Protein: 11 g

Ingredients: artesian well water, lentils, carrots, tomato paste, celery, mirepoix soup base (sautéed vegetables, soybean oil, sea salt, natural flavours), onion, natural flavours, tamari, parsley, evaporated cane juice, garlic, sea salt, spices

Format: frozen

Remarks: all organic, wheat-free, kosher, microwaveable

Split Pea Soup
Serving size: 213 g

Protein: 12 g

Ingredients: artesian well water, split peas, carrots, mirepoix soup base (sautéed vegetables, soybean oil, sea salt, natural flavours), onions, evaporated cane juice, natural flavours, tamari, honey, garlic, spices

Format: frozen

Remarks: all organic, wheat-free, kosher, microwaveable

Yves Veggie Cuisine
Veggie "Neatballs"

Serving size:	60 g
Protein:	13 g
Ingredients:	water, soy protein product, vital wheat gluten, soy protein, wheat protein product, canola oil, dextrose, tapioca starch, salt, natural flavour, yeast extract, malt extract, spices, carrageenan (from seaweed), vitamins and minerals
Format:	refrigerated
Remarks:	no GM foods

Tofu Dogs

Serving size:	38 g
Protein:	9 g
Ingredients:	water, soy protein, vital wheat gluten, tofu (water, soybeans, magnesium chloride), yeast extract, salt, wheat starch, organic evaporated cane juice, cold-pressed canola oil, spices, carrageenan (from seaweed), natural liquid smoke, beet root powder, wheat germ, vitamins and minerals
Format:	refrigerated
Remarks:	no GM foods

Veggie Breakfast Links

Serving size:	50 g
Protein:	11 g
Ingredients:	water, soy protein, vital wheat gluten, natural flavour, soy protein product, evaporated cane juice, tapioca starch, wheat protein product, carrageenan (from seaweed), salt, spices, beet root powder, vitamins and minerals
Format:	refrigerated
Remarks:	no GM foods

Veggie Breakfast Patties

Serving size: 57 g

Protein: 11 g

Ingredients: water, soy protein product, vital wheat gluten, natural flavour, cold-pressed canola oil, carrageenan (from seaweed), yeast extract, soy protein, malt extract, organic evaporated cane juice powder, salt, vegetable gum, potato starch, konjac flour, vitamins and minerals

Format: refrigerated

Remarks: no GM foods

Canadian Veggie Bacon

Serving size: 38 g

Protein: 11 g

Ingredients: water, vital wheat gluten, soy protein, soy protein product, natural flavour, spices, yeast extract, salt, gum arabic, rice starch, beet root powder, carrageenan (from seaweed), locust bean gum, guar gum, evaporated cane juice, wheat germ, natural liquid smoke, vitamins and minerals

Format: refrigerated

Remarks: no GM foods

Hot 'n' Spicy Chili Veggie Dogs

Serving size: 52 g

Protein: 13 g

Ingredients: water, soy protein isolate, vital wheat gluten, organic evaporated cane juice, cold-pressed canola oil, spices, salt, natural flavour, yeast extract, carrageenan (from seaweed), tomato paste, natural liquid smoke, citric acid, vitamins and minerals

Format: refrigerated

Remarks: no GM foods

Veggie Chili

Serving size: 300 g

Protein: 21 g

Ingredients: water, red kidney beans, tomatoes, onions, soy protein product, red peppers, green peppers, carrots, tomato paste, spices, wheat protein product, natural flavour, salt, organic evaporated cane juice, yeast extract, malt extract, carrageenan (from seaweed), wheat germ, oat bran, rice starch, beet root powder, vitamins and minerals

Format: refrigerated

Remarks: no GM foods

Veggie Penne

Serving size: 300 g

Protein: 12 g

Ingredients: water, tomatoes, penne pasta, roasted red peppers, onions, soy protein product, tomato paste, burgundy wine, wheat protein product, roasted garlic, salt, spices, organic evaporated cane juice, cornstarch, cold-pressed olive oil, natural flavour, malt extract, citric acid, carrageenan (from seaweed), sesame oil, vitamins and minerals

Format: refrigerated

Remarks: no GM foods

Veggie Lasagna

Serving size: 300 g

Protein: 17 g

Ingredients: water, tomatoes, mafalda pasta, tomato paste, onions, soy protein product, natural flavour, wheat protein product, organic evaporated cane juice, garlic, cornstarch, spices, cold-pressed olive oil, salt, malt extract, carrageenan (from seaweed), vitamins and minerals

Format: refrigerated

Remarks: no GM foods

Veggie Ground Round (Italian, Original)

Serving size: 55 g

Protein: 10 g

Ingredients: water, soy protein product, wheat protein product, natural flavour, malt extract, salt, spices, organic evaporated cane juice, carrageenan (from seaweed), wheat germ, oat bran, vitamins and minerals

Format: refrigerated

Remarks: no GM foods

Veggie Pizza Pepperoni

Serving size: 48 g

Protein: 14 g

Ingredients: water, soy protein, vital wheat gluten, spices, tofu (water, soybeans, magnesium chloride), salt, natural flavour, organic evaporated cane juice, cold-pressed canola oil, wheat starch, yeast extract, beet root powder, guar gum, natural liquid smoke, carrageenan (from seaweed), vitamins and minerals

Format: refrigerated

Remarks: no GM foods

Veggie Dogs

Serving size: 46 g

Protein: 11 g

Ingredients: water, soy protein isolate, vital wheat gluten, yeast extract, salt, wheat starch, evaporated cane juice, spices, carrageenan (from seaweed), beet root powder, natural liquid smoke, wheat germ, vitamins and minerals

Format: refrigerated

Remarks: no GM foods

Veggie Salami Slices

Serving size: 62 g

Protein: 17 g

Ingredients: water, vital wheat gluten, soy protein, tofu (water, soybeans, magnesium chloride), spices, salt, wheat starch, natural flavour, organic evaporated cane juice, yeast extract, beet root powder, natural liquid smoke, carrageenan (from seaweed), vitamins and minerals

Format: refrigerated

Remarks: no GM foods

Veggie Bologna Slices

Serving size: 62 g

Protein: 15 g

Ingredients: water, soy protein, vital wheat gluten, spices, canola oil, organic evaporated cane juice, natural flavour, salt, yeast extract, carrageenan (from seaweed),wheat starch, rice starch, beet root powder, wheat germ, citric acid, vitamins and minerals

Format: refrigerated

Remarks: no GM foods

Veggie Chick'n Burger

Serving Size: 85 g

Protein: 17 g

Ingredients: water, soy protein product, vital wheat gluten, cold-pressed canola oil, natural flavour, spices, yeast extract, carrageenan (from seaweed), salt, vegetable gum, organic evaporated cane juice, lemon juice powder, potato starch, konjac flour, vitamins and minerals

Format: refrigerated

Remarks: no GM foods

Garden Vegetable Patties

Serving size: 85 g

Protein: 11 g

Ingredients: water, soy protein product, brown rice, onions, carrots, rye flakes, green beans, peas, vital wheat gluten, red pepper, tomato paste, corn, soy protein, yeast extract, vegetable gum, natural flavour, organic evaporated cane juice, spices, salt, carrageenan (from seaweed), potato starch, konjac flour, citric acid

Format: refrigerated

Remarks: no GM foods

Veggie Burger

Serving size: 85 g

Protein: 17 g

Ingredients: water, soy protein product, vital wheat gluten, wheat protein product, cold-pressed canola oil, natural flavour, organic evaporated cane juice, carrageenan (from seaweed), salt, malt extract, spices, yeast extract, vegetable gum, potato starch, konjac flour, beet root powder, vitamins and minerals

Format: refrigerated

Remarks: no GM foods

Black Bean and Mushroom Burger

Serving size: 85 g

Protein: 12 g

Ingredients: water, soy protein product, black beans, corn, onions, brown rice, vital wheat gluten, spices, tomato paste, yeast extract, wheat protein product, carrageenan (from seaweed), natural flavour, pea fiber, guar gum, salt, mushrooms, soy protein, sweet red pepper granules, malt extract, lemon juice powder, citric acid

Format: refrigerated

Remarks: no GM foods

Zoglo

Crispy Meatless Cutlets

Serving size: 83 g (1 cutlet)

Protein: 14 g

Ingredients: textured soy protein, water, wheat gluten, vegetable oil, dried egg white, beet fibre, spices, salt, dried onion, natural flavour, hydrolyzed vegetable protein, ferrous fumarate, vitamin B_{12}, niacin, thiamin, pantothenic acid, pyridoxine hydrochloride, riboflavin

Format: frozen

Remarks: kosher

Meatless Mini Loaves

Serving size: 90 g

Protein: 18 g

Ingredients: textured soy protein, water, wheat gluten, vegetable oil, dried egg white, beet fibre, spices, salt, dried onion, natural flavour, ferrous fumarate, vitamin B_{12}, niacin, thiamin, pantothenic acid, pyridoxine hydrochloride, riboflavin

Format: frozen

Remarks: kosher

Meatless Chicken-Flavour Patties

Serving size: 75 g (1 patty)

Protein: 15 g

Ingredients: textured soy protein, water, wheat gluten, vegetable oil, dried egg white, beet fibre, spices, salt, dried onion, natural flavour, hydrolyzed vegetable protein, ferrous fumarate, vitamin B_{12}, niacin, thiamin, pantothenic acid, pyridoxine hydrochloride, riboflavin

Format: frozen

Remarks: kosher

Savoury Meatless Wieners

Serving size: 76 g

Protein: 13 g

Ingredients: textured soy protein, water, wheat gluten, vegetable oil, dried egg white, beet fibre, spices, salt, dried onion, natural flavour, iron and B vitamins

Format: frozen

Remarks: kosher

Savoury Meatless Kebabs

Serving size: 80 g

Protein: 16 g

Ingredients: textured soy protein, water, wheat gluten, vegetable oil, dried egg white, beet fibre, spices, salt, dried onion, hydrolyzed vegetable protein, natural flavour, iron and B vitamins

Format: kosher

Remarks: frozen

Golden Meatless Nuggets

(contains 10–12 chicken-flavour nuggets)

Serving size: 72 g (4 nuggets)

Protein: 12 g

Ingredients: textured soy protein, water, wheat gluten, vegetable oil, dried egg white, beet fibre, spices, salt, dried onion, natural flavour, hydrolyzed vegetable protein, ferrous fumarate, vitamin B_{12}, niacin, thiamin, pantothenic acid, pyridoxine hydrochloride, riboflavin

Format: frozen

Remarks: kosher

Some Good Resources for Your Kitchen Library

Cooking Light. P.O. Box 1748, Birmingham, Alabama.
Both of us subscribe to this magazine, which is full of wonderful ideas every month. The editorial team and consultants are dietitians, nutritionists, and physicians, which adds to the magazine's credibility. This publication combines the latest nutritional information, in the form of short articles, with simple, tasty, healthy recipes.

Jenkins, N. H. *The Mediterranean Diet Cookbook.* Bantam, 1994.
A culinary tour of the Mediterranean, unveiling the tastes of France, Italy, Greece, Tunisia, Lebanon, Spain, Cyprus, Turkey, Morocco, and more. This book, following the spirit of the famous Mediterranean diet, offers a wide range of cultural and nutritional information. It's practically bedside reading!

Madison, D. *This Can't Be Tofu!* New York: Broadway Books, 2000.
A hundred and fifty-five pages of simple — and less simple — ideas, always very tasty, for cooking tofu. The author makes masterful use of the spices and herbs in her pantry. A book to discover!

Madison, D. *Vegetarian Cooking for Everyone*. New York: Broadway Books, 1997.
Deborah Madison received the Julia Child Cookbook Award for this book: 725 pages of delightful flavours, with 1,400 recipes using vegetables, fruits, whole grains, legumes, and soy. If you like adventure, this book will be a voyage of discovery and a celebration of delicious plant foods. "Whatever recipe I try, I know that it will be delicious and will please both my palate and my health!" (LD)

Sass, L. *The New Soy Cookbook*. San Francisco: Chronicle Books, 1998.
If you want to explore cooking with tempeh and tofu, Lorna Sass offers new paths. About 120 pages of recipes, good photographs, and relevant suggestions.

Shurleff, W., and A. Aoyagi. *The Book of Tofu*. Berkeley: Ten Speed Press, 1983.
If you want to know about tofu from A to Z, including how to make all varieties of tofu, this is the book for you. It's a gold mine of information and includes a range of incredible recipes. If you're developing a love for tofu, you must buy this book!

Some useful resources on vegetarianism

Davis, B., and V. Melina. *Becoming Vegan*. Summertown, TN: Book Publishing Company, 2000. The essential reference for everyone who wants to become a strict vegetarian or vegan. Written by two vegan dietitians internationally known for their nutritional and scientific knowledge, this book provides information and motivation to eat better without having recourse to foods of animal origin.

Melina, V., B. Davis, and V. Harrison. *Becoming Vegetarian*. Summertown, TN: Book Publishing Company, 1995. This 275-page book supplies all the answers about different types of vegetarianism in light of the most recent nutritional research. It addresses questions about health and prevention and even gives good tips on eating in restaurants or at friends' houses.

Bibliography

Adlercreutz, H. "Western Diet and Western Diseases: Some Hormonal and Biochemical Mechanisms and Associations." *Scandinavian Journal of Clinical Laboratory Investigation*, 50 (1990): 3–23.

American Diabetes Association. "Position Statement: Nutrition Recommendation and Principals for People with Diabetes Mellitus." *Diabetes Care*, 22, Suppl. 1 (1999): S42–S45.

American Dietetic Association. "Position Statement: Phytochemicals and Functional Foods." *Journal of the American Dietetic Association*, 95 (1995): 493–96.

——. "Position Statement: Vegetarian Diets." *Journal of the American Dietetic Association*, 97 (1997): 1317–21.

Anderson, J. W., et al. "Meta Analysis of the Effects of Soy Protein Intake on Serum Lipids." *New England Journal of Medicine*, 333 (1995): 276–82.

Appel, L. J., et al. "Effect of Dietary Patterns on Serum Homocysteine: Results of a Randomized, Controlled Feeding Study." *Circulation*, 102 (2000): 852–57.

Bagchi, D. "Bioflavonoids and Polyphenols in Human Health and Disease Prevention." *Nutrition & the M.D.*, 25, no. 5 (1999).

Barnard, N., et al. "Effectiveness of a Low-fat Vegetarian Diet in Altering Serum Lipids in Healthy Premenopausal Women." *American Journal of Cardiology,* 85 (2000): 969–72.

Barnes, S. "Role of Soy in Cancer Prevention and Treatment."
Web site: <www.soyohio.org/health/diet/cancer.htm> Sept. 2000.

Bradley, S., and R. Shinton. "Why Is There an Association between Eating Fruit and Vegetables and a Lower Risk of Stroke?" *Journal of Human Nutrition and Dietetics,* 11 (1998): 363–72.

Brand-Miller, J. C. "The Importance of the Glycemic Index in Diabetes." *American Journal of Clinical Nutrition,* 59, suppl. (1994): 747s–52s.

Chandalia, M., et al. "Beneficial Effects of High Dietary Fibre Intake in Patients with Type 2 Diabetes Mellitus." *New England Journal of Medicine,* 342 (2000): 1392–98.

Chester, E. A. "Soy for Cardiovascular Indications." *American Journal of Health System Pharmacology,* 58 (2001): 660–63.

Conlin, P. R., et al. "The DASH Trial." *American Journal of Hypertension,* 13 (2000): 949–55.

Constantinou, A. J., et al. "Consumption of Soy Products May Enhance the Breast Cancer Preventive Effect of Tamoxifen." *Proceedings of the American Association for Cancer Research* (2001): 42.

Crouse, J. R., et al. "A Randomized Trial Comparing the Effect of Casein with that of Soy Protein Containing Varying Amounts of Isoflavones on Plasma Concentrations of Lipids and Lipoproteins." *Archives of Internal Medicine,* 159 (1999): 2070–76.

Frenz, M. J., et al. "Nutrition Principles for the Management of Diabetes and Related Complications." *Diabetes Care,* 17, no. 5 (1994).

Gao, G., et al. "Increases in Human Plasma Antioxidant Capacity after Consumption of Controlled Diets High in Fruit and Vegetable." *American Journal of Clinical Nutrition,* 68 (1998): 1081–87.

Greenwood, S., et al. "The Role of Isoflavones in Menopausal Health: Consensus Opinion of the North American Menopause Society." *Menopause,* 7 (2000): 215–29.

Health Canada, Health Protection Branch, Laboratory Centre for Disease Control. *Heart Disease and Stroke in Canada.* 1997.
Web site: http://www.hc-sc.gc.ca/hpb/lcdc/bcrdd/hdsc97/s06_f.html.

Heany, R. P., et al. "Bioavailability of the Calcium in Fortified Soy Imitation Milk, with Some Observations on Method." *American Journal of Clinical Nutrition,* 71 (2000): 1166–69.

"Homocysteine and Cardiovascular Disease." *Nutrition & the M.D.*, 25, no. 11 (1999).

Horiuchi, T., et al. "Effect of Soy Protein on Bone Metabolism in Postmenopausal Japanese Women." *Osteoporosis International*, 11 (2000): 721–24.

Hu, F. B., et al. "Frequent Nut Consumption and Risk of Coronary Heart Disease in Women: A Prospective Cohort Study." *Journal of Nutrition*, 129 (1999): 1135–39.

Iwamoto, M., et al. "Walnuts Lower Serum Cholesterol in Japanese Men and Women." *Journal of Nutrition*, 130 (2000): 171–76.

Jenkins, D., et al. "The Effect on Serum Lipids and Oxidized Low-density Lipoprotein of Supplementing Self-selected Low-fat Diets with Soluble-fibre, Soy and Vegetable Protein Foods." *Metabolism*, 49 (2000): 67–72.

Joshipura, K., et al. "Fruit and Vegetable Intake in Relation to Risk of Ischemic Stroke." *Journal of the American Medical Association*, 282 (1999): 1233–39.

Kendall, C., and D. Jenkins. "Les bienfaits du soya pour la santé." Insert in *Revue canadienne de la pratique et de la recherche en diététique*, 61 (Winter 2000).

Kipel, K. F., and K. C. Ornelas. *The Cambridge World History of Food.* Cambridge University Press, 2000.

Krause, R. M., et al. "Dietary Guidelines, Revision 2000: A Statement for Healthcare Professionals from the Nutrition Committee of the American Heart Association." *Circulation*, 102 (2000): 2284–89.

Kris-Etherton, P., et al. "Lyon Diet Heart Study: Benefits of a Mediterranean-style, National Cholesterol Education Program/American Heart Association Step 1 Dietary Pattern on Cardiovascular Disease." *Circulation*, 103 (2001): 1823–25.

Lamartinière, C. A. "Protection against Breast Cancer with Genistein: A Component of Soy." *American Journal of Clinical Nutrition*, 71, suppl. (2000): 1705–07.

Lascheras, C., et al. "Mediterranean Diet Beneficial for Elderly Subjects." *Nutrition Research Newsletter*, 19 (2000): 14–15.

Leaf, A. "Dietary Prevention of Coronary Heart Disease: The Lyon Diet Heart Study." *Circulation*, 99 (1999): 733–35.

Li, D., et al. "Effect of Dietary α-linolenic Acid and Thrombotic Risk Factor in Vegetarian Men." *American Journal of Clinical Nutrition*, 69 (1999): 872–82.

Liebman, B. "Plants for Supper? 10 Reasons to Eat More Like a Vegetarian." *Nutrition Action Newsletter*, 23 (1996): 10–12.

Lissin, L. W., et al. "Phytoestrogens and Cardiovascular Health." *Journal of the American College of Cardiology*, 35 (2000): 1403–10.

Liu, S., et al. "Fruit and Vegetable Intake and Risk of Cardiovascular Disease: The Women's Health Study." *American Journal of Clinical Nutrition*, 72 (2000): 922–28.

Liu, S., et al. "A Prospective Study of Whole Grain Intake and Risk of Type 2 Diabetes Mellitus in U.S. Women." *American Journal of Public Health*, 90 (2000): 1409–15.

——. "Whole Grain Consumption and Risk of Ischemic Stroke in Women: A Prospective Study." *Journal of the American Medical Association*, 284 (2000): 1534–40.

Lorgeril, M. de, et al. "Mediterranean Diet, Traditional Risk Factors, and the Rate of Cardiovascular Complications after Myocardial Infarction: Final Report of the Lyon Diet Heart Study." *Circulation*, 99 (1999): 779–85.

Loria, C. M. "Serum Folate and Cardiovascular Disease Mortality among U.S. Men and Women." *Journal of the American Medical Association*, 160 (2000): 3258–62.

Lu, L. J. W., et al. "Screening and Prevention of Breast Cancer." *Cancer Research*, 60 (2000): 4112–21.

——. "Soy Consumption May Reduce Breast Cancer Risk." American Association for Cancer Research, Annual Meeting presentation, Philadelphia, 12 April 1999.

McDonald, B. "The awesome power of the humble flax seeds." Report, National Institute of Nutrition, 13, no. 3 (1998).

McMichael Philipps, D. F., et al. "Effects of Soy Protein Supplementation on Epithelial Proliferation in the Histologically Normal Human Breast." *American Journal of Clinical Nutrition*, 68, suppl. (1998): 1431s–36s.

Meltze, S., et al. "Lignes directrices de pratique clinique 1998 pour le traitement du diabète au Canada." *Canadian Medical Association Journal*, 159, suppl. (1998): S1–S32.

Messina, M. J. "Legumes and Soybeans: An Overview of their Nutritional Profiles and Health Effects." *American Journal of Clinical Nutrition*, 70, suppl. (1999): 439s–450s.

——. "Soy, Soy Phytoestrogens (Isoflavones) and Breast Cancer" (letter). *American Journal of Clinical Nutrition*, 70 (1999): 574–75.

Morgan, W. A., et al. "Pecans Lower Low Density Lipoprotein Cholesterol in People with Normal Lipid Levels." *Journal of the American Dietetic Association*, 100 (2000): 312–18.

Murkies, A., et al. "Phytoestrogens and Breast Cancer in Postmenopausal Women: Case Control Study." *Menopause*, 7 (2000): 289–96.

Omenn, G. S., et al. "Preventing Coronary Heart Disease: B Vitamins and Homocysteine" (editorial). *Circulation*, 97 (1998): 421–24.

Ontario Soybean Growers' Marketing Board. *Canadian Soyfoods Directory*. 1997.

Porrini, M., et al. "Absorption of Lycopene from Single or Daily Portions of Raw and Processed Tomato." *British Journal of Nutrition*, 80 (1998): 353–61.

Potter, S., et al. "Soy Protein and Isoflavones: Their Effects on Blood Lipids and Bone Density in Postmenopausal Women." *American Journal of Clinical Nutrition*, 68, suppl. (1998): 1375s–79s.

Rendall, M. "Dietary Treatment of Diabetes Mellitus" (editorial). *The New England Journal of Medicine*, 342 (2000): 1440–41.

Robertson, R. M., and L. Smaha. "Can a Mediterranean-style Diet Reduce Heart Disease?" (editorial). *Circulation*, 103 (2001): 1821–22.

Sabate, J. "Nut Consumption, Vegetarian Diets, Ischemic Heart Disease Risk and All-cause Mortality: Evidence from Epidemiologic Studies." *American Journal of Clinical Nutrition*, 70, suppl. (1999): 500s–3s.

Somekawa, Y., et al. "Soy Intake Increases Bone Mass in Postmenopausal Women." *Obstetrics and Gynecology*, 97 (2001): 109–15.

"Soy Protein Health Claim Gets FDA Authorization." *Nutrition & the M.D.*, 25, no. 11 (1999).

Steinmetz, K. A., and J. D. Potter. "Vegetables, Fruit and Cancer Prevention: A Review." *Journal of the American Dietetic Association*, 96 (1996): 1027–39.

Stephen, A. M., and M. Lal, for the National Institute of Nutrition. "The role of grains in the Canadian diet." *Le Point I.N.N.*, 14, no. 2 (1999).

Tikkanen, M. J., et al. "Effect of Soybean Phytoestrogen Intake on Low Density Lipoprotein Oxidation Resistance." *Proceedings of the National Academy of Science USA*, 95 (1998): 3106–10.

Vegetarian Dietetic Practice Group of the American Dietetic Association, Isoflavones. *Vegetarian Nutrition*. 1999.

Vincent, A., and L. A. Fitzpatrick. "Soy Isoflavones: Are They Useful in Menopause?" *Mayo Clinic Proceedings*, 75 (2000): 1174–84.

World Cancer Research Fund and American Institute for Cancer Research. *Food, Nutrition and the Prevention of Cancer: A Global Perspective.* Washington, DC: American Institute for Cancer Research, 1997.

Xu, X., et al. "Soy Consumption Alters Endogenous Metabolism in Postmenopausal Women." *Cancer Epidemiological Biomarkers Prevention*, 9 (2000): 781–86.

Zava, D. T., et al. "Estrogenic and Antiproliferative Properties of Genistein and Other Flavonoids in Human Breast Cancer Cells in Vitro." *Nutrition and Cancer*, 27 (1997): 31–40.

Index